Great Questions of the Bible

Fred M. Wood

Broadman Press
Nashville, Tennessee

4281-31 (BRP edition)
4219-43 (paperback edition)
ISBN: 0-8054-1943-8

Printed in the United States of America

All Scripture quotations, unless otherwise indicated, are from the Revised Standard Version.

Scripture quotations marked "Goodspeed" are from *The New Testament, an American Translation,* Edgar J. Goodspeed.

Scripture quotations marked "Moffatt" are from *The Bible, a New Translation,* James Moffatt.

Scripture quotations marked "Phillips" are from *The New Testament in Modern English,* © J. B. Phillips, 1958. Used with permission of The MacMillan Company.

Scripture quotations marked NEB are from *The New English Bible* © The Delegates of the Oxford University Press, and the Syndics of the Cambridge University Press 1961, 1970. Reprinted by permission.

Affectionately dedicated
to
Mrs. Mary Catherine Gibson

Who, for more than twenty years, served faithfully and devotedly
as my secretary at Eudora Baptist Church

Preface

The pessimists of our day have overwhelmed us with their world views of hopelessness and despair. They have told us that man is a lonely atom condemned to be a prisoner in the cell of the universe. They have spoken of man's complete helplessness before our mechanical civilization—the cruelty of our bureaucratic world.

Is this the final word? Can man find purpose and fulfillment in our day, or is all hope for meaning only a futile quest?

Whatever else we may say of Christianity and of Jesus Christ, he intended for us to live victoriously in this world. Although he died at thirty-three, he is still the most triumphant person who ever lived. Even the cross, the instrument of his death, has become a symbol of conquest. More than anything else, we need to be gripped by his spirit and challenged by his life. With Jesus Christ, we can face the darkest hours victoriously. Without him, life has us defeated forever.

These are simple questions—but vital ones. They are

concerned with our relationship with Christ, our involvement with his church, and our philosophy toward life and its problems. We *can* be victorious even in our despairing world.

"The victory that defeats the world is our faith" (1 John 5:4, NEB). In fact, this faith of ours is the only way in which the world has been conquered. "For who could ever be said to conquer the world but the man who really believes that Jesus is God's Son?" (1 John 5:4-5, Phillips)

Contents

1. Where Are You? 9
2. Am I My Brother's Keeper? 17
3. What Is in Your Hand? 25
4. Who's on the Lord's Side? 33
5. Why Do You Serve God? 42
6. Why Do Bad Men Prosper and Good
   Men Suffer? 50
7. Do You Agree with God? 57
8. What Is Man? 64
9. What Do You Do More Than Others? 72
10. What Are You Looking For? 79
11. What Is a Life Worth? 86
12. What Is a Saved Man's First Prayer? 93
13. What Do You Think of Your Church? 101
14. Four Questions with the Same Answer 110
15. What Do You Think of Jesus? 118

1. Where Are You?

"But the Lord God called to the man and said to him, 'Where are you?'" (**Gen. 3:9, NEB**).

Did you ever tune in during the middle of a television program with a complicated plot? Although frustrating, it can be intellectually challenging as you try to imagine forward and guess backward at the same time.

It's already late in the story when we look at this question, Where are you? Quite a bit has taken place. A beautiful garden—sinless people—a subtle suggestion: "You won't die. God doesn't love you. He's afraid you'll be as smart as he is." And Eve believed it! Deep in our hearts we all want to be God and will believe almost any lie that promises us position and status.

Next came the rude awakening. The morning after always brings reality and remorse!

> Slight was the thing I bought,
> Small was the cost I thought;
> Poor was the loan at best,
> God—but the interest!
> —PAUL LAURENCE DUNBAR

The eyes of both Eve and her husband were opened, and

9

they knew they were naked. They sewed fig leaves together for aprons!

They Heard the Voice

The voice always comes because conscience makes cowards of us all. We can temporarily fool our consciences and sometimes do a good job of it. Kant, the philosopher, spoke of the two great wonders of God's creation—the starry heavens above and the moral law within. Freud replied with tongue in cheek: "The stars are unquestionably superb, but where the conscience is concerned, God has been guilty of an uneven and careless piece of work." The conscience may be good, or it may be bad. It all depends upon how we nurture and train it. The same marvelous faculty that guides us along the road to morality can also act as a sadistic slave driver, a self-accusing fury, and a tireless jobber in guilt. Also, never forget that we may rationalize and whitewash it until we have convictions as spineless as a jellyfish.

Guilt always hears a voice! A young girl sat in a minister's office. She unloaded into his listening ears a full confession of an affair with an older man. After being assured no one knew or suspected, she exclaimed: "Thank God! I feel that everyone who sees me can read it in my face!"

God Always Walks

Wherever we are, he is there. The psalmist says,

> Where could I go from thy
> Spirit,
>   where could I flee from thy
> face?
> I climb to heaven?—but thou
> art there;

10

> I nestle in the nether-
>   world?—and there thou art!
> If I darted swift to the dawn,
>   to the verge of ocean afar,
> thy hand even there would fall
>   on me,
> thy right hand would reach
>   me.   •
> If I say, "The dark will screen
>   me,
>   night will hide me in its cur-
>   tains,"
> yet darkness is not dark to thee,
>   the night is clear as daylight.
> >   (Ps. 139:7-12, Moffatt)

He is always there. He gives assurance with his presence.
An unknown author has written:

> There is an eye that never sleeps
> Beneath the wing of night,
> There is an ear that never shuts
> When sink the beams of light.
>
> There is an arm that never tires,
> When human strength gives way;
> There is a love that never fails
> When earthly loves decay.

Sometimes he is there to give protection. "The eternal
God is your refuge and dwelling place, and underneath are
the everlasting arms" (Deut. 33:27). Often, he may be there
to rebuke—to chastise his own and call them back to duty.
"Jonah rose to flee to Tarshish from the presence of the
Lord. He . . . found a ship going to Tarshish . . . and went

11

on board. . . . But the Lord hurled a great wind upon the sea" (Jonah 1:3-4).

Not As Before

In this story the Lord is represented as "walking in the garden." The almost casual manner in which this is stated indicates it did not occur just then for the first time. The assumption that God had repeatedly done this is quite feasible. In other words, man and woman had previously enjoyed periods of fellowship with their Creator. Sin had not driven a wedge between them and their Maker. There was the sweet communion of those who shared mutual ideals and attitudes. What is more beautiful than the sweet spirit which comes through loving fellowship?

But now it is different! The old intimacy is gone. There is an immense spiritual distance between the creature and the Creator. There are many ways we can break with those whom we love. Friendship may be lost through *neglect.* The writer of Proverbs says, "A friend loves at all times. There are friends who pretend to be friends" (Prov. 17:17; 18:24). If we fail to care in the time of need, we can lose the sweet fellowship that was once present.

Friendship may be lost by *finding other interests.* We grow away from some things and some people. We do not argue and separate. We merely separate. Do you remember the sign in the office that read: "Don't go away mad. Just go away!" Sometimes, as here, communion is broken through *lack of gratitude*—taking for granted favors and friendships. Shakespeare said:

> Blow, blow, thou winter wind,
> Thou art not so unkind

As man's ingratitude:

....

Freeze, freeze, thou bitter sky
Thou dost not bite so nigh
    As benefits forgot.

No human relationship, fellowship, or friendship, though, is quite comparable to the divine-human encounter. No earthly friend has the unqualified claim upon a person as does the heavenly Father. He is sovereign. He alone is capable of loving with a pure and unselfish love. God is, therefore, within his rights when he says, "Thou shalt not." We may have baser motives when we forbid or prohibit a friend from a deed or when we seek to secure an action from him. We may do it to dominate in order to feed our ego, but God does it for our good. He knows the "thou shalt not" will help us attain the good life.

Things are different now in the garden! Man is estranged. He is separated from pure love. God is changed for man. No longer is he companion and joy-bringer. Now he is policeman. Man must hide. Sin has taken its toll. Frederick William Faber wrote:

There is not one evil that sin has not brought me
There is not one good that has come in its train

Sin makes things different—always worse.

Why Does He Come?

Beyond a doubt, God requires that we periodically take inventory. Every child of God needs to reexamine himself constantly. Eternal vigilance is the price not only of liberty but also of maintaining the best in every realm of endeavor.

Where are you, Christian? Are you a better person than

a year ago? Are you kinder? Are you more unselfish? Do you care more for others? Or have you alienated yourself from God through disobedience? Does some moral short-coming make life miserable? Have you cheated, lied, gossiped, hated? Do you feel a sympathetic identification with the one who testified as to sin's devastating effect,

> So long as I refused to own my guilt,
>   I moaned unceasingly, life ebbed away;
> for thy hand crushed me night and day,
>   my body dried up, as in the summer heat.
>   (Ps. 32:3, Moffatt)

If this is you, there is but one word. Jesus said it to a church that had lost the warmhearted love with which it started, "Repent and do the works you did at first" (Rev. 2:5). God told Jacob to arise and go back to Bethel. Why Bethel? This was where he first met his God and made vows to him—vows that had been broken for many years. We do not, however, outgrow the memories. We do not lose the capacity for being affected by the powers that once influenced us. The first man and woman sinned, but they did not lose God—his voice continued to haunt and to call. The leaves of gathering years can never cluster so thickly that we shall cease to hear God's voice, "Where are you, O child, where are you?"

He Calls to Claim

If we would understand the call, we must see the purpose. God is the great Seeker. He does not come merely to chastise and discipline but to claim us as his own. He is constantly searching for the last, the least, the lost. This is the glory of Christianity, the full flower of Judaism's bud. Jesus is

14

a seeking Savior. He leaves the ninety and nine and goes out into the wilderness. There is more rejoicing over the one who is saved than the ninety and nine who are safe. He is the Son of man who came to *seek* and to save. Do you know the basic difference between Christianity and other religions? Religion is man seeking a God. Christianity is God seeking a man.

> I sought the Lord, and afterward I knew
>> He moved my soul to seek Him, seeking me;
> It was not I that found, O Savior true;
>> No, I was found of Thee.

> Thou didst reach forth Thy hand and mine enfold;
>> I walked and sank not on the storm-vexed sea;
> 'Twas not so much that I on Thee took hold
>> As Thou, dear Lord, on me.

> I find, I walk, I love, but O the whole
>> of love is but my answer, Lord, to Thee!
> For Thou wert long beforehand with my soul,
>> Always Thou lovedst me.

Why does God do it? Because he cannot leave his creation. The psalmist said: "Know that the Lord is God! / It is he that made us, and we are his; / we are his people, and the sheep of his pasture" / (Ps. 100:3). God cannot leave his own. Hosea shouted, "How can I give you up, O Ephraim! / How can I hand you over, O Israel!" / (Hos. 11:8) The prophet's cry is not interrogation but exclamation—not a question but a quandary. He cannot do it. God is grace. Love is not merely an attribute of God. It is his essence.

The novelist Thackeray and three friends were out walking one day. On the Dean Road, west of Edinburgh they passed a quarry and saw a large wooden crane standing out above it in the sky. It looked exactly like a cross. Thackeray stopped, pointed, and said one word softly, "Calvary." They all moved on silently and deep in thought. Why would a man such as he, not really a deeply spiritual man, do and say this? James Stewart says: "It is because man . . . has always been conscious that there, in that cross God has spoken . . . we know that past all our human efforts . . . here is God's answer."

Where are you? Have you been to Calvary for the cleansing power? Are you living near to him who lived for us, died for us, and lives again and forever for us? The hymn writer Elizabeth Clephane said:

> I take, O Cross, thy shadow
>   For my abiding place;
> I ask no other sunshine than
>   The sunshine of His face;
>
> Content to let the world go by,
>   To know no gain or loss,
> My sinful self my only shame,
>   My glory all the cross.

Where are you?

2. Am I My Brother's Keeper?

"Then the Lord said to Cain, 'Where is Abel your brother?' He said, 'I do not know; am I my brother's keeper?' " (Gen. 4:9).

An old truism says, "God made the country, but man made the cities." Man made some other things, also. He introduced the human race to such jarring disharmonies as rebellion, greed, jealousy, hatred—and murder. Someone has suggested Cain did not plan to kill. He was angry. His feelings had been hurt. "I didn't realize . . . I'm sorry . . . I didn't mean to . . . ." *But Abel was dead.*

How many times the story is that simple. I didn't know . . . I should have been more careful . . . What was I thinking about? *But the deed is done.* James declares, "So when a man knows what is right and fails to do it, he is guilty of sin" (Jas. 4:17, Goodspeed).

Watch Sin Grow

No man is an island. He cannot live to himself. Whether or not we like it, or even admit it, we are bound together in a bundle of life. In a remarkable way, we are shaped and molded by each other and we mold each other. We can never be solitary, isolated persons. What we do affects

17

others—especially those we love. Sin began as a single act. Eve ate. Then it became a husband-wife affair. She gave to her husband, and he ate also. Now the child is about the same business. When will parents learn that "you can't kid the kids."

Tennyson said, "Nothing ever dies." It grows both in extent and degree. First the vertical relationship between man and God is severed. Next, the horizontal relationship between man and man is broken. Ralph Murray says: "That which first paralyzed Adam's power to look *up* has now paralyzed Cain's power to look *out*. . . . The sin of rebellion has become the sin of murder! How fast the venom . . . spreads."

The acceptance of it by us grows. There was a time when our standards were high and conscience's voice was clear. Gradually, however, we have moved. First, we refused to be intolerant and narrow-minded. We smiled politely. After all, we didn't want to lose friends—or customers. Second, a small participation would make us more acceptable and not hurt too much. Finally, we switched sides. Alexander Pope wrote:

> Vice is a monster of such frightful mien,
>> That, to be hated, needs but to be seen;
> But seen too oft, familiar with its face,
>> We first endure, then pity, then embrace.

A Difference in Worship

Men have differed through the years—sometimes quite vociferously—concerning the best way to know and worship God. Correct doctrine is important, of course, but few, if any, people are debated into the kingdom of God. Life, not strife, tells of Jesus. Deeds, not creeds, show the true nature of our Savior.

> From your eye He beckons me,
> And from your heart His love is shed;
> Till I lose sight of you and see
> The Christ instead.

Some go to great lengths to trace the "scarlet thread" of redemption through the Old Testament. Some follow those first-century Christians who allegorized and typified every Old Testament passage in sight which would help prove that Jesus of Nazareth was the promised Messiah. These people point out that Abel's worship had the shedding of blood as the essential element. Does not the writer of Hebrews say, "Without the shedding of blood there is no forgiveness of sin"? (Heb. 9:22)

Others feel this is pushing a good teaching too far—further than necessary in order to believe in redemption. It was, they say, Abel's attitude of faith in God. The quality of his devotion was apparent, and the Lord approved his worship because it was validated by his righteous life and godly deeds.

B. H. Carroll, and others, have insisted that the emphasis was on the quantitative nature of the gifts. Abel brought the "firstlings of the flock" as an offering. The first tenth, says Carroll, not the last tenth, belongs to God. The first part is that which is holy unto him.

The indisputable truth, whatever the reason, is that God was pleased with Abel and his offering. Cain was angry. God rebuked him for his sour attitude. Cain refused to be corrected. He met Abel in the field, discussed the situation, and killed his brother. Times haven't changed. We still will forfeit everything in life rather than admit we've made a mistake. We fight back rather than give in. We vent our hostilities against innocent victims. We strike out at the innocent and pour misery, our misery, upon them. When will we learn?

We Kill in Many Ways

When Jesus interpreted the Old Testament code of conduct, he went far beyond the deed. He spoke of motive. He that is angry with his brother is in danger. The trouble begins when the twisted idea finds root in the mind and begins to fertilize. A famous lawyer once said: "Everybody is a potential murderer. I have not killed anyone, but I frequently get satisfaction out of the obituary notices." Too often we hate people not for what they do but for what they are. One of Shakespeare's characters says, "His life has a daily beauty that makes me ugly."

Often we list those things that kill—slander, poisonous gossip, harsh and hurting words—but indifference can crush as quickly, even more so. A kind word might have helped greatly. It could have given meaning to life—encouragement—a desire to keep on in the face of difficulty and disappointment. But we didn't bother to speak. We were busy—preoccupied with self. We just didn't take time. This is also something that kills.

> When Jesus came to Birmingham,
> We merely passed Him by;
> We didn't hurt a hair of Him,
> We only *let* him die.
>
> For men had grown more tender,
> They would not give Him pain;

They merely passed Him down the street,
And left Him in the rain.[1]

Our blundering folly or icy indifference can give wounds that are too deep for healing. The methods of murder are many.

Are We Responsible?

How far does God go in putting our brother on our shoulders? Aren't we individuals, and isn't the glory of Christianity found in its emphasis on individualism? Don't we have our own life to live? Is it so wrong to plan wisely and provide for our own needs so as not to be dependent upon society? Quite often our brother doesn't want our help or concern. After all, we can't be chasing around "sticking our nose" into someone else's business, can we?

To ask these questions, however, is but to answer them when we remember the words and deeds of Jesus. He went where they were, made himself available to meet their needs. A woman by the well—a man in a sycamore tree—a blind man by the side of the road—Jesus believed they were his responsibility. He put himself there so as to be of service to them. The conclusion is inescapable. A Christian must be concerned about the welfare of his brother.

In our day we have sought more subtle ways to avoid our obligations. We have programmed and institutionalized our helpful deeds and benevolent activities. We are too busy. Here's a check. Let the agencies handle this problem. Humanitarianism has become one of the biggest income producing businesses in the nation! Surely we care! We gave 18 percent of our income to charitable causes last year! Best of all, it's deductible!

21

The Most Important

All areas of concern are important, but some are more meaningful than others. We help our brother most when we introduce him to Jesus. We must feed him if he is hungry and clothe him when he is naked. This is a presupposition. If he is not given more than bread and clothes, however, he will soon be hungry and naked again. Jesus brings new motivation because he gives a reason for living. He gives a peace concerning guilt, concerning death, and concerning the life to come. When one is safe and secure in these areas, life takes on new meaning.

Neither can we delegate our mission work. Unless we love the near one, we do not love the far one. It's easy to love the one across the ocean. This is noble and idealistic—also it requires so little. An Englishman challenges us and stings a little, too:

> Oh, how I love Humanity
> > With love so pure and pringlish,
> And how I hate the horrid French,
> > Who never will be English!
> The International Idea,
> > The largest and the clearest,
> Is welding all the nations now,
> > Except the one that's nearest.
> This compromise has long been known,
> > This scheme of partial pardons,
> In ethical societies
> > And small suburban gardens.
> The villas and the chapels where
> > I learned with little labour
> The way to love my fellow-man
> > And hate my next-door neighbor.

It Is Our Business

Jesus reminded his parents when they found him in the Temple, "Did you not see and know that it is necessary (as a duty) for Me to be in My Father's house, and [occupied] about My Father's business?" (Luke 2:49, Amplified Bible) We, too, have a supreme duty. It is to be about our Father's business, and the greatest area of service is to take the gospel of God's redeeming grace to those who are enslaved by sin. Nothing is more important!

Often, people are indifferent to their own spiritual need. We can become discouraged when they make no response to our efforts. To refrain from bitterness is difficult, but if we are to be good witnesses, we must display the sweet spirit of our Savior who continued to love and to labor even when he was rejected or ignored. Ezekiel understood the duty of God's people toward their fellow man. He said,

> Now, son of man, I have placed you as a sentinel for Israel; whenever you hear a word from my lips, warn them from me. When I tell the wicked, "You must die,"—then, if you do not say a word of warning to the wicked to give up his evil course, he has to die for his iniquity, but I will hold you responsible. Yet if you warn the wicked to give up his evil course and if he will not give it up, he has to die for his iniquity, but you have saved yourself (Ezek. 33:7-9, Moffatt).

The matter is settled. We are our brother's keeper. What he does and where he stands in relationship to his Maker is our business. Many stories have been told of John Vassar, the dedicated soul-winner of another generation. Once, while in the lobby of a fashionable hotel, he talked with a woman obviously wealthy and sophisticated. He asked her about her spiritual welfare and her love for the Savior. Her husband returned as Mr. Vassar was leaving. He asked his wife, "What was that man talking to you about?" She replied, "He asked me if I were a Christian." The man demanded very pompously, "Why didn't you tell him that it was none of his business?" "I started to tell him that," she said, "Really I did. But if you could have seen the concern in his eyes and heard the tenderness of his voice, I think you would have agreed that it seemed that it was his business—and that he was doing and saying the thing that was exactly right for him to do and say."

Fanny J. Crobsy wrote:

> Down in the human heart,
> Crush'd by the tempter,
> Feelings lie buried
> That grace can restore;
> Touch'd by a loving heart,
> Waken'd by kindness,
> Chords that are broken
> Will vibrate once more.

Cain's question, "Am I my brother's keeper?" is answered by Jesus, "You shall love your neighbor as yourself" (Matt. 22:39). It is answered, also, by Paul who said, "I have, in short, been all things to all sorts of men that by every possible means I might win some to God" (1 Cor. 9:22, Phillips).

3. What Is in Your Hand?

"The Lord said unto him 'What is that in your hand?'" (*Ex. 4:2*).

What do you do when you see something you don't understand? People have various reactions. Some immediately turn away from it and refuse to be interested. Some criticize, claiming it is wicked. Some react as the old-timer who saw a giraffe for the first time. He looked with amazement and said, "There ain't no such animal!" Moses saw something he had never seen before—the bush was burning with fire, but the bush was not consumed.

Often, we find God in unlikely places. Since we speak so often of the beauty of God's presence, we forget that he can be seen in other experiences. He can be found in adversity—in the wildernesses of life. Helen Keller said: "I thank God for my handicaps for through them I have found myself, my work, and my God."

Of course, if we are to see God in life's experiences, we must be looking for him. Many people were upset a few years ago when the Russian cosmonaut said that he scanned the skies and did not anywhere see God. One man replied that a person who speaks like this would also say, "I have

25

examined the brain and nowhere do I see a mind." The natural man does not understand spiritual things. Elizabeth Barrett Browning insists;

> Earth's crammed with heaven,
> And every common bush afire with God;
> And only he who sees takes off his shoes;
> The rest sit around it and pick blackberries.

A Forty-Year Shortcut

Moses was one of the first in a long line who have tried the shortcut to success. His mother must have whispered to him many times during the years at the palace, "God will send a leader to free his people from slavery and oppression." Moses decided God was calling him to do it—and now! Why wait? One day he saw an Egyptian oppressing a Hebrew. Moses killed the Egyptian and hid his body in the sand. Moses thought no one knew of it, but how wrong he was! Our secret sins are seldom as secret as we think! The next day a fellow Hebrew shattered his illusions, "Who made you a prince and a judge over us?" (Ex. 2:14)

This pushed the panic button! Everybody knows it! I'll get out of town! The shortcut turned out to be the long, hard way. It usually does. Shortcuts can be uppercuts! For forty years Moses labored for his father-in-law. His visions of grandeur crumbled into the dust.

Much must be left unsaid about those long years of service in the backside of nowhere. The hotheaded, impulsive young man cooled off. He almost completely forgot those youthful dreams and resigned himself to "growing old gracefully"—perhaps bitterly. This happens frequently when we run ahead, not of God's will, but of his time schedule. Marjorie

Allen Anderson wrote:

> Impatient hearts want action—now!
> They fear God's time will be too late;
> How prone we are to rush ahead—
> When God says, "Wait!"

God's Hour Comes

One of God's prophets said, "For still the vision awaits its time; / it hastens to the end—it will not lie. / If it seems slow, wait for it; / it will surely come, it will not delay" (Hab. 2:3). One day God will be ready for us—ready to put us in the place of service he has chosen for us. A seminary professor used to pray, "Lord prepare us for the place of labor you are preparing for us."

Not all of God's calls are so dramatic—few are. But they all are important—urgent since they are from him.

Moses may have become rebellious, but more likely he was merely defeated, frustrated, and ready to resign from the game of life. Someone has said, "Impression without expression leads to depression." Once, Moses was sure of God's plan for his life. Then he became not so sure. Now, he had lost the spark. He was mistaken about the whole thing. Life's bottom had fallen out. All inspiration was gone. Have you ever been there? An unknown writer said:

> No vision and you perish;
> No ideal and you're lost;
> Your heart must ever cherish
> Some faith at any cost.

> Some hope, some dream to cling to,
> Some rainbow in the sky,
> Some melody to sing to,
> Some service that is high.

God was now ready. He felt Moses was willing to come in humility and let the Lord lead. One thing, however, was wrong. Moses had lost all interest in the cause. Which is the worse course of action—to run ahead of God or to drag behind? It's a bitter choice. An unknown author wrote:

But hearts debate and question God
Our hesitating feet are slow,
We yield to cautious reasoning
When God says, "Go!"

Humility or Hardheadedness?

What was involved in the reluctance of Moses to serve? Was he naturally humble? Did he, therefore, recoil from such a tremendous undertaking? Did he refrain from accepting the responsibility because he knew the magnitude of the task? Let us remember Moses had been brought down a long way. Alexander Maclaren says, "Looking after sheep in the desert was a sad downcome from the possibility of sitting on the throne of Egypt." Quite often those who volunteer too eagerly drop out too quickly.

On the other hand, all that poses as humility is not the genuine product. It can be hardheaded unwillingness wearing a disguise. In all probability, there was a little of both in the episode of the burning bush!

Who am I? Whom shall I say is sending me? They will not believe me! I cannot talk well! God had an answer for each excuse. You are important for God will be with you. Tell them of the eternal God of their fathers. What is in your hand? Throw it on the ground! Pick it up! Did you realize the power you may have when you are obedient to God and his will? I'll touch your tongue, or I'll even get you a spokesman—Aaron, your brother. But, later, Moses never allowed Aaron to speak very much! He was much like the minister who begged the church for an assistant pastor and then would not ever let him preach.

What was the real problem? Moses just did not want to do the job. He cried, "Oh, my Lord, send, I pray, some other person" (Ex. 4:13). An unknown writer paraphrased a hymn:

I'll go where you want me to go, dear Lord,
I'll say what you want me to say,
But I'm busy right now for myself, dear Lord,
I'll help you some other day.

Moses didn't promise to help any other time. He merely refused to accept the job. Was he humble or hardheaded?

Surrender at Last

Why did Moses finally agree to go? His last excuse was answered by a promise that Aaron would be his spokesman. The text is not clear but perhaps this did the job. The Lord must have seen Moses' willingness for he added, "And you shall take in your hand this rod, with which you shall do the signs" (Ex. 4:17). Did Moses suddenly realize God might take even more of the leadership away from him if he continued to offer excuses? In fact, God might give the whole job to Aaron if Moses didn't accept the proposition.

Do you remember the story of the lady who was very sick. She called her husband to the bedside and said: "I'm about to die and I want to make a suggestion. You're going to need someone to look after you when I'm gone. I think the widow Jones down the street would make you a good wife after I die." Her husband said: "I've been thinking about that, too. I believe you're right." What happened?

That lady got well—in a hurry!

Moses didn't tell Jethro the full story of the burning bush. In fact, he didn't mention it at all. He merely said he was going to Egypt in order to see his family. It is never a good policy to tell people too much of our intimate relationships with the Lord. When Jesus came down from the mount of transfiguration with the disciples he said, "Tell no one the vision" (Matt. 17:9).

Why should we hold our visions sacred? Why should we refuse to traffic or barter cheaply with them? For one thing, they are precious, because they are few and far between. Also, visions can be understood only by those who are spiritually prepared for them. We only lessen the power of the vision when we try to tell the uninitiated of it. Most important, however, visions dissipate when we talk too much about them. Frederick Reinartz says: "Like rose bushes, they cannot stand much exposing of their roots. And visions, like electrical energy, must be passed through insulated wires, so that when they are called upon to deliver light and power they will not have been dissipated in sputtery, flashy short circuits. These sometimes blow fuses and cut off all power." Robert Browning makes Saul say concerning his vision:

> Oh, could I tell, you surely would believe it,
> Oh, could I show what I myself have seen,
> How can I tell, and how can you receive it,
> How till he bringeth you where I myself have been?

What Do You Have?

Now, let's talk about *you*. What possibilities lie within your personality? Are you using them for God? All of us have talents that can be dedicated and will be multiplied if they are turned over to him. One minister tells of seeing a man standing outside a very sophisticated place of amusement. He was greeting the guests—a sort of public relations man. He thought how fine it would be to have a man of this ability greeting his visitors on Sunday morning and Sunday night before the worship and preaching service. This man was won to Christ and became chief usher in the minister's church. How much was in that man's hand!

Of course, it takes hard work to develop our talents. The road is not easy. The best leaders are those who will train for their jobs. A young lady once said to an accomplished pianist, "I'd give anything if I could play the piano like that." He replied, "Would you give eight hours of practice a day for thirty years?"

God is asking us as he did Moses, "What is in your hand?" These words rebuke those who think God can use only men of outstanding gifts. Actually, not many men of so called "worldly wisdom" find their place of service in God's kingdom. When God calls, they are usually not within "hearing distance." We should never long wistfully for greater gifts. The most successful person in God's cause is the obedient one. Any sincerely dedicated person is great in God's sight. Outstanding ability is not the prime requisite. Willingness, sincerity, dedication—these are the essential matters—the determination to obey and follow God at all cost. James Hastings says: "What is in thine hand? Do not be deterred from handing it back to God because it is so little. What we have is what the Lord wants. What we are he has made us—and for this hour."

Moses, what is in thy hand?
    Only a shepherd's crook,
A weak, frail stick for guiding sheep,

But Moses! Moses! Look!
It has become a living thing!
    And henceforth from this hour
Dedicated to our God
    It symbolizes power.

Samson, what is in thy hand?
    Only a bleached bone,
Left upon the field to rot,
    But with this alone,
Dedicated to our God
    A thousand foes are slain
A nation's heart is turned to God
    And peace is made to reign.

David, what is in thy hand?
    Only a little sling
From which I often cast small stones,
    But with this alone,
Dedicated to our God
    A giant is brought low!
A nation's heart revives again
    And vanquished its foe.

Christian, what is in thy hand?
    Some simple, little thing?
Some gift neglected—e'en despised?
    Still, if you will bring
Your gift, and lay it at His feet,
    Nor wait—this very hour,
Dedicated to our God,
    Your mite becomes a power.
                  —AUTHOR UNKNOWN

4. Who's on the Lord's Side?

"Moses stood in the gate of the camp and said, 'Who is on the Lord's side? Come to me'" (*Ex. 32:26*).

When a group of people are without wise direction, they can get into trouble quickly! Unless unusually mature, an unshepherded congregation can easily fly off on a tangent and come up with unbelievably wild schemes. An organization moves forward upon the wings of those who guide it. In most cases, those who criticize strong leadership would secretly like to be "calling the signals" but would probably make a mess of the situation if they were put in charge of it.

Moses was on the mountain receiving the Law from the Lord. This experience is recorded in Exodus 19—20. The remainder of Exodus is concerned with extended legislation concerning God's way of life for his people. Most of these laws were given directly to Moses while he was on top of Mt. Sinai. The Ten Commandments were inscribed on tablets of stone by the finger of God.

The Value of Solitude

Do you like to be alone? Samuel Johnson once said that

the greatest business of his life was to escape from himself. There is much to be gained from the quiet times. Jesus went apart often to pray and rest. We live in a busy world. If we are wise, we will retire periodically and spend silent times with ourselves and God. Many people will testify that the greatest victories of their life have been possible because they have developed what Wordsworth described as:

> that inward eye
> Which is the bliss of solitude.

While Moses was alone with God, the great laws for Hebrew life were given to him. The great moments of vision and understanding God's purposes likewise come to us most often when we are alone with him. Alfred North Whitehead said, "Religion is what a man does with his solitariness." There are rooms of deepened insight whose doors remain locked and thresholds of spiritual growth which remain uncrossed until we shut out the world and feast on the valuable and rare luxury of rich fellowship with God.

> I needed the quiet, so He drew me aside
> Into the shadows where we could confide;
> Away from the bustle where all the day long
> I hurried and worried when active and strong.
>
> I needed the quiet, though at first I rebelled,
> But gently, so gently, my cross He upheld;
> And whispered so sweetly of spiritual things;
> Though weakened in body, my spirit took wings
> To heights never dreamed of when active and gay,
> He loved me so gently, He drew me away.
>
> I needed the quiet, no prison my bed,
> But a beautiful valley of blessing instead:

A place to grow richer, in Jesus to hide,
I needed the quiet, so He drew me aside.

Moses went up into the mountain to be with his Maker and to come back with a mind of pure and lofty thoughts, a heart of happy memories and an earnest purpose to give himself more completely in God's service. We also can be motivated for effective and dynamic living when we spend quiet moments apart from the world.

The Crowd Below

The scene changes! While the cat's away the mice have a "ball." When strong spiritual discipline is removed, the animal nature reasserts itself.

They are always there—these foxes that spoil the vineyard. Soon they become roaring lions. Man is forever forgetting his Creator and making a god in his own image. The people saw that Moses delayed, and they became restless! It's the same old story today. In our religious life we know how to run but not how to walk!

"We can't wait on Moses! Come on Aaron, make us some gods to lead us. There's no telling what has happened to Moses by now." The leader was absent and the assistant yielded to the clamor of the people. Aaron said to them, "Break off the golden earrings from the ears of your wives and sons and daughters, and bring them to me" (Ex. 32:2, Moffatt). He took them and carved them with a tool into a metal calf. The people then began to worship, erecting an altar in front of the golden calf. They proclaimed a feast of worship for the next day. They brought offerings, sat down to the feast, and then rose to amuse themselves in singing, dancing, and revelry.

35

What a strange thing is idolatry! The ancients gave concrete examples of expression to their idolatry by giving names, carving statues, and erecting altars to certain values or thoughts which might dominate a man's life. For instance, man did not worship wine, as such, but he conceived a god of wine whom he called Bacchus and worshiped this god. Power was personified in the god of power named Zeus. Wisdom was personified in Minerva and love in Venus. The word *Mammon* was the Chaldee, Syriac, and Punic name for the god of things or money. The modern man is too sophisticated to say he is dedicated to Bacchus or Mammon. This would be admitting idolatry. Instead he enjoys his cocktail parties and burns out all his energies seeking to make and pile up wealth.

It is difficult for us to recognize idolatry when we see it. We associate idolatry with stones and metal images. In reality, a man's idol is that idea, concept, or value which is the controlling factor in his life and which occupies his time, dominates his thoughts, and claims his loyalty. Duke McCall says: "The most tragic sight on the American horizon is the smoke rising from the altars of ambition, lasciviousness, and wealth. On these altars are being sacrificed family, friends, character, and health. The very mother who is nauseated by the account of a Hindu mother casting her baby into the River Ganges to satisfy some pagan idol may be at the moment sacrificing her own daughter's soul upon the altar of her social ambition."

Righteous Indignation

One of the most accurate guides to a person's character is that which arouses his disgust. Tolerance is a great virtue—up to a point. There are times when silence is golden, but there are other times when it is plain "yellow." A British author once said in an interview, "The tribute I am most eager to deserve is one that would say I am among those who will not take evil good naturedly." Halford Luccock contends that the good causes of this earth have their greatest obstacles not in the enemies who fight them as in the alleged friends who do not care.

Moses never took evil "good naturedly." He cared deeply. When he saw the revelry and dancing, he reacted immediately. The Bible says: "Moses blazed out in anger; he flung down the tablets and broke them . . . he took the calf they had made and burned it up, grinding it to powder, which he threw into water and made the Israelites drink it" (Ex. 32:19-20, Moffatt).

A word of caution is necessary for us at this point. The Lord reminds us that punishment for sin is in his hands. We are to leave punitive measures to God. Paul says, "Vengeance is mine, I will repay, says the Lord" (Rom. 12:19). We cannot go around "blowing our top" indiscriminately at anyone who disagrees with our approach to godliness and call it defending the faith. Perhaps you have heard of the man who was told by his psychiatrist that he should not repress his natural feelings. If someone irritated him, he should tell the person in no uncertain terms that his conduct was offensive. Later, much wiser, he wrote:

> Psychiatrists advise us
> That we should blow off steam
> Should let our tempers have full play
> Should stomp our feet and scream.
>
> I thought I would try this plan—
> Just let my true self go—

Results were quick in coming,
As the following doth show:

A stranger bumped me on the street,
I muttered, "Stupid creature!"
At church next day, I rued my word—
The man was our new preacher.

A phone call got me out of bed,
I answered sharp and cross
How was I supposed to know
The caller was my boss?

It may relieve our tensions
To speak out now and then . . .
But doctors who advise it
Should also tell us WHEN.

There will always be conflicts between basic value systems. We cannot tear to shreds those who disagree with us, but we must take our stand for the things in which we believe—not with hatred and hostility but with firmness tempered by a loving spirit and a winsome personality. It isn't easy!

He Loved His People

This Old Testament story is one which brings mingled emotions to those of us who know the New Testament ethic. First, Moses demanded that the people positionize themselves. He shouted: "Who is on the Lord's side? Come to me" (Ex. 32:26). Next, he gave a command for the sons of Levi to go throughout the camp and put to death those who were leaders in the defection from God's way of holiness. About three thousand men were killed. Then Moses

38

went up into the mountain to pray for the people. We see, in his prayer, one of the greatest intercessory petitions to be found in the history of religion: "Alas, this people have sinned a great sin. . . . But now, if thou wilt forgive their sin—and if not, blot me, I pray thee, out of thy book which thou hast written" (Ex. 32:31-32).

Only one other prayer compares with it. Paul exclaimed: "I am speaking the truth in Christ, I am not lying . . . I have great sorrow and unceasing anguish in my heart. For I could wish that I myself were accursed and cut off from Christ for the sake of my brethren, my kinsmen by race" (Rom. 9:1-3).

It is not easy to have this double attitude. Yet everyone who loves properly must have it. Discipline for the wrong; love and a refusal to cast off the wrongdoer! Every parent knows it! Every real leader of people knows it! We are often impatient with, even intolerant of, imperfection in others yet we continue, at all cost, to be their friend and their counselor.

Where Are You?

This story is no mere incident from the early years of Hebrew history. It is alive with meaning for us. The forces of sensual indulgence are still in conflict with those of personal discipline. The fool still says, "Eat, drink, and be merry" while the healthy and well-ordered personality knows that only in stabilized self-control can true happiness be found.

What about you? Have you learned this great lesson? There are times when the greatest source of character development is to wait for God's own good time. Our activistic world clamors for gratification of every whim immediately.

39

Granger Westberg reminds us that the word *discipline* is derived from the word *disciple*. He says: "A disciple is one who is willing to be disciplined by his leader or the master who loves the disciple in a mature and constructive way. This is one of Christianity's basic premises." We cannot have everything we want immediately. Sometimes we must wait. This can be difficult.

> There are days of silent sorrow
> In the seasons of our life,
> There are wild, despairing moments,
> There are hours of mental strife;
> There are times of stormy anguish
> When the tears refuse to fall
> But the waiting time, my brothers,
> Is the hardest time of all.
> —SARAH DOUDNEY

Having made due allowance for the necessity of patience, let us underscore one further point clearly. There comes a time when we must make a choice, as James Russell Lowell wrote:

> In the strife of truth with falsehood
> For the good or evil side.

Who is on the Lord's side? Moral neutrality is inexcusable. In fact, it is impossible. We are made for decisions and loyalties—not to balance ourselves between alternatives. To refuse to choose the right is to side with those forces which oppose the right. A law in ancient Greece said that if a revolution should break out in the streets those who merely looked on without taking sides were to be put to death. Man has a duty as a citizen to make his contribution to the moral forces of the day in which he lives. It is a crime to be a mere spectator in the battle of life.

God's children also have a responsibility to choose sides. Sometimes the choice will be between good and evil. Other times it may be between merely the good and the best. It can be that we have time to consider deliberately the options, or the moment of decision may be thrust upon us calling for an immediate verdict. The same one who said, "Who's on the Lord's side?" also plead later, "I have set before you life and death . . . choose life that you and your descendants may live" (Deut. 30:19).

Where is your loyalty?

5. Why Do You Serve God?

"Has not Job good reason to be God-fearing?" (*Job 1:9, NEB*).

When one first reads of Job's righteousness and his great wealth, he immediately says: "Here is the person I've been looking for—a man who is both pious and prosperous. What possible fault can be found with him?" The cynic, however, is perennially present. He is one whose idealism has turned sour. Knowing the price of everything but the value of nothing, he can always find a basis for criticism and usually wastes no time puncturing the tire of every genuinely good action performed by a sincerely dedicated man of God.

The accuser is Satan! The very name means "adversary" and a descriptive title indeed! There are two major approaches of the carping critic. Sometimes he uses a blunt instrument, such as a meat-ax, and does his work crudely with chopping methods. At other times, however, he uses skill and finesse. Often a simple question adroitly put forth is sufficient. If he cannot discount the obvious godliness of the person, he can devaluate the worth of the conduct by raising a doubt as to the motive which prompts the action.

The One Accused

The target for the jibes of Satan is Job. This ancient patriarch had fabulous wealth. His personal possessions consisted of seven thousand sheep, three thousand camels, five hundred yoke of oxen and five hundred she asses. He is described as "the greatest of all the people of the east" (1:3).

In addition, Job's family was a source of joy to him. Seven sons and three daughters! Even today, most people would think the proportion of male to female was virtually ideal! The fellowship among the grown children was a delight to the parents. The men took turns entertaining in their homes, and they always invited their sisters to be with them.

This greatly blessed man was a person of personal devotion and of many good deeds. Each day, as his children feasted, Job prayed for them. He did it in case they had "sinned and cursed God in their hearts" (1:5). Eliphaz testified to Job's actions as a good neighbor: "You have strengthened the weak hands. Your words have upheld him who was stumbling, and you have made firm the feeble knees" (4:3-4).

By whatever yardstick we might care to measure Job, he would rank high. He was an A plus student in the school of moral and ethical standards. It is easy to understand why God could say, "Have you considered my servant Job, that there is none like him on the earth, a blameless upright man, who fears God and turns away from evil?" (1:8).

Hate Will Find a Way

An old cliche says, "Love will find a way." Quite often, though, the opposite is also true. If one searches thoroughly, he can find a weak place in the strongest character. A girl once said about another whom she disliked: "I didn't say I despise her. I just said the only polish she has is on her fingernails." Satan personifies all that is devilish in this universe. He is man's enemy, his adversary, his accuser. As he wanders around, kicking up the stardust, he has a smirk on his face. Harboring criticism in his heart, he rolls it around as a sweet morsel on his tongue. He despises God, God's moral government, and anyone who seeks to live in harmony with the principles of righteousness. Pictured as a sour sophisticate, he has been all over the earth, going to and fro, walking up and down in it (2:2). He is the true critic, believing every man will sell out if the stakes are high enough.

The Subtle Question

Satan is forever raising doubts about righteousness and righteous people. To Eve he inquired, "Did God say?" (Gen. 3:1). To Jesus he challenged, "If you are the Son of God" (Matt. 4:3). To the Lord, he slyly suggested, "Does Job fear God for nought?" (1:9).

Is this question fair? Of course not! Does Satan ever play by the rules of good sportsmanship? How far can any man go in art for art's sake, truth for truth's sake, or good for goodness' sake? The matter of rewards and punishments is always inextricably interwoven within the fabric of our motivations.

Several questions rear their heads as we consider Satan's accusations. Is there in existence such a thing as disinterested righteousness? If there were no heaven, would you still want to be a Christian? If extinction were your inevitable end, would you be willing to accept all the disciplines of the

Christian faith? As the story of Job unfolds, other similar questions are raised. Will a man be faithful to his godly convictions when dishonor, pain, and even disgrace seem to be the result of his righteousness? Would one even be willing to go to hell for the glory of God? Which is the stronger motive, uninformed righteousness or informed selfishness? These are not ancient and irrelevant interrogations from another civilization. They are as contemporary as tomorrow morning's sunrise.

Motivation Analyzed

A new science has arisen in recent years called motivation research. Why do we act as we do in given situations? These experts discovered some years ago a woman would pay $2.50 for a jar of skin cream but only 25¢ for a bar of soap. Why? Soap only promised to make her clean. The cream promised to make her beautiful. So, today soaps promise beauty as well as cleanliness. One executive says that the women are buying a promise. The experts go on to say: "People do not buy orange juice. They buy vitality. Cosmetic manufacturers do not sell lanolin. They sell hope. Man does not buy an automobile. He buys prestige."

Although Jesus emphasized the inner thought much more than the outward act, Christians have said little, until recently, about the motive which prompts the deed. Look at the volumes of anthologies which have flooded the market. They have quotations from the great writers on all the important subjects. Yet, notice the paucity of statements on the matter of motive. Why have we shied away from this subject? Have we been afraid to look deeply within lest we see something we do not like? When Henry Van Dyke, however, listed his four things a man must do, he did not overlook it.

> Four things a man must learn to do,
> If he would keep his record true;
> To think without confusion clearly
> To love his fellow man sincerely
> To act from honest motives purely
> To trust in God and heaven securely.[1]

It Isn't Easy

To keep our motives completely pure is difficult, perhaps impossible. Do you remember the story of the preacher's son whose father had received a call to a larger, more lucrative, church? Someone asked him, "Is your daddy going to accept the church?" He replied: "I'm not sure yet. Pop's upstairs praying, and Mom's downstairs packing."

Neither is the layman exempt from professional attitudes and improper motivations. What is the basic reason many have for tithing their income to the Lord's work through the church? Far too often, it is a secret fear that the Lord will "collect" it some other way if they fail to give it willingly. Closely connected with this is the often felt belief that profits will be better if the tenth is sent to the church—a sort of immunization against adversity.

A minister was once addressing a group of rural preachers in a summer retreat for pastors. He was pointing out to them that it was much nearer to the spirit of the New Testament to tell people they should bring their tithes and offerings because they love the Lord and his work than to threaten them that if they did not do so the Lord might kill their best cow. One preacher replied, "I guess that's true all right. But it sure takes the teeth out of some of my sermons." A faithful layman once said to his pastor:

"There are many ways the Lord can pour out a blessing to a couple besides giving more material possessions. He can give them a happy home and children who are faithful Christians." It takes deep insight and sincere humility (not the false kind) to be true and honest with oneself.

What Is the Answer?

Actually, there is no absolutely unerring solution to the problem of pure motives. We know in part, and we perform in part. All of our motives are mingled. George Buttrick says, "Our best intentions are streaked with base alloy—but they are not all base! Education by violence may still educate."

How far can we go in serving God through fear? Let us be honest. Most of us became Christians through the motivation of fear. We did not want to die and go to hell. We, therefore, repented of sin and received Jesus as Savior. This is a legitimate motive. Jesus warned, "How are you to escape being sentenced to hell?" (Matt. 23:33). Paul said, "Knowing the fear of the Lord, we persuade men" (2 Cor. 5:11). As we grow older in years and in Christian maturity, we recognize that the motivation must be deeper if service is to maintain continuity. The Christian life must become the life of love. John said: "There is no room for fear in love; perfect love banishes fear. For fear brings with it the pains of judgment, and anyone who is afraid has not attained to love in its perfection" (1 John 4:18, NEB). Phillips paraphrases these words: "Love contains no fear—indeed fully-developed love expels every particle of fear, for fear always contains some of the torture of feeling guilty."

How can we love supremely? How can our love become the constraining force for dynamic devotion? The answer is our love is not adequate of itself. It can never be. Paul said, "For the love of Christ controls us" (2 Cor. 5:14). William Hersey David used to insist to his Greek classes, "This is the subjective genitive, not the objective genitive. It is not our love for him that motivates but rather his love for us."

> My love is oft times low,
> My joy still ebbs and flows;
> But peace with Him remains the same,
> No change my Saviour knows.
> I change: He changes not,
> God's Christ can never die;
> His love not mine, the resting place,
> His truth, not mine, the tie.
>
> —HORATIUS BONAR

When our fellowship with Christ becomes so meaningful and selfless that it is based on love and love alone, we may understand the spirit of the great mystic of the Middle Ages who said:

> My God, I love Thee, not because
>   I hope for heaven thereby,
> Nor because they who love Thee not
>   Are lost eternally.
>
> Not with the hope of gaining aught,
>   Not seeking a reward,
> But as Thyself hast loved me,
>   O ever loving Lord,
>
> E'en so I love Thee and will love,
>   And in thy praise will sing,
> Solely because Thou art my God,

And my Eternal King,

and can testify with another child of God:

> O Christ, Love's Victim, hanging high
>   Upon the cruel Tree,
> What worthy recompense can I
>   Make, mine own Christ, to Thee?
>
> My toil and labour from this day,
>   My whole life, let it be,
> To love Thee aye the best I may
>   And die for love of Thee.

Did Job fear God for nothing? Do you?

6. Why Do Bad Men Prosper and Good Men Suffer?

"Why does the way of the wicked prosper? Why do all who are treacherous thrive?" (Jer. 12:1).

The boyhood life of Jeremiah was a sheltered one. His family was a priestly group—the descendants of Abiathar. They had been exiled to Anathoth because Abiathar sided with Abijah against Solomon in the struggle for David's throne at his death. More than three centuries later this family still maintained its identity and was ministering about spiritual things in the small village only a few miles from Jerusalem.

When Jeremiah began preaching, good king Josiah was on the throne. These two men showed many common interests—one of the greatest was zeal for the law of Moses. The king sponsored a revival of obedience to the law. One of the chief planks in his platform was abolishing the local places of worship in the rural sections and centralizing worship at the Temple in Jerusalem. In most cases this was an excellent action. Perverted and even immoral types of worship often arose at these "high places" or isolated shrines.

Josiah sent Jeremiah on a preaching tour throughout the

circuit round about Jerusalem. One of his assignments was his hometown, Anathoth. With youthful zeal, he urged the people to tear down the local shrines and come to Jerusalem to worship Jehovah. His hometown folk, including some of his own family, did not share his zeal. A conspiracy arose against him, and he was treated shamefully, nearly killed. The young boy awoke to reality and poured out his heart to God in complaint.

> Why do bad men prosper?
> > why are scoundrels secure and serene?
> Thou plantest them and they take root,
> > they flourish, yes and they bear fruit!
> Thou art always on their lips,
> > but far, far from their hearts
> > > (Jer. 12:1-2, Moffatt).

Have you ever asked this question? Do you sometimes feel God is unfair in his administration of justice? Do you wonder why the good people seem to suffer while the wicked people always win? Let us examine the matter.

It Isn't Always True

In the first place, " 'taint necessarily so." There are many examples of good people becoming wealthy and sinful people suffering dreadfully. Murderers in some countries are executed. Thieves go to jail. Drunkards become alcoholics and lose all their possessions. It happens regularly. On the other hand, Christian laymen build big businesses and become faithful stewards of their money. Some of the most successful people in the history of America's economic expansion have been men thoroughly devoted to the cause of Christ.

51

The moral law of sin and death operates—just as accurately and unyielding as any of the so-called "laws of nature." We do not break God's laws but rather destroy *ourselves* when we violate them. Dr. Hersey Davis used to say, "We do not break the law of gravity when we jump off the twentieth floor of an office building—we only demonstrate it." Paul, in his letter to the Romans, tells how God gives up to their own vileness those who, because of their lusts, have bartered away the true God for a false one, degrading their bodies and plunging their misguided minds into darkness. Make no mistake about it—the wages of sin is death!

There is another law at work in the world—the "law of the spirit of life in Christ Jesus." Born-again people have been rescued by Christ from the law of sin and death and transplanted into the realm where the law of love operates. This is what Christianity is all about. Only spiritually born people understand spiritual things. Paul wrote, "Those who live on the level of our lower nature have their outlook formed by it . . . but those who live on the level of the spirit have the spiritual outlook" (Rom. 8:5, NEB).

These two laws operate! A life lived in harmony with righteousness will be beautiful and find fulfillment. Washington Gladden learned a great lesson and wrote about it. He discovered and testified

> In the darkest night of the year
> When the stars are all gone out
> That courage is better than fear
> That faith is truer than doubt.
>
> And fierce through the fiends may fight
> And long though the sun may hide,

I know that truth and right
Have the universe on their side.

But Often It Is True

If life were completely systematized and logically arranged, we would have no problem in understanding why things happen as they do. Unfortunately, however, the sinner doesn't always receive a just recompense in this world. Sometimes he prospers greatly. Contrariwise, some of the godliest men and women alive are called on to suffer most. Is God fair?

Habakkuk saw this and complained about it to God. As he observed the wicked condition of Judah's day, he said:

Oh thou Eternal, how long shall I cry,
    and thou wilt never hear?
I complain to thee of wrongs
    and yet thou wilt not help.
....
                outrage and injury go on,
till strife is stirred and faction;
and so Law is benumbed,
justice is never in action—
for evil men hamper the just,
till justice go awry
                (Hab. 1:2-4, Moffatt).

In marriage relationships, we see this happen. A faithful wife suffers for years at the hand of an overbearing, tyrannical husband. Mild, meek men are made miserable by frustrated, domineering, overbearing females. Sickness comes to the godly while the wicked enjoy good health. In the business world, employees cringe in terror before a demanding supervisor. Dedicated Christians lose their jobs or miss the promotion while the most ungodly or immoral man in the company is made division manager. The sweet Christian mother with three children loses her husband at thirty while the thrice divorced girl of twenty-eight marries a wealthy widower and becomes financially secure. It just isn't fair! No wonder Jeremiah shouted concerning the men who were causing him anxiety and even bodily suffering: drag them away like sheep to the slaughter, devote them to their day of doom (Jer. 12:3, Author's translation).

Are There Answers?

The problem of suffering will not be solved in a few moments. James Stewart devotes four sermons to it in one book. Leslie Weatherhead's book, *Why Do Men Suffer,* has 224 pages. George Buttrick's *God, Pain and Evil* contains 235 pages, and he had thirty books on the subject before him as he wrote. If the answer could be solved completely, surely the solution would have been discovered by now. But a few suggestions are in order.

For one thing, *God disciplines his own children.* He is obligated to do so. He has no obligations to discipline Satan's family. Who comprises God's family? It is those who have been twice born. A lady once asked the writer: "Why do I who am a Christian—though a weak and worldly one many times, I admit—have so many problems and backsets? Look at my neighbor. She doesn't even pretend to be a Christian, but she does well—very well." What was the answer? "Lady, whose children do you spank? Yours or your neighbor's?" Before further explanation could be offered, she said; "I see it. You don't have to explain any further."

The writer of Hebrews says, "My son regard not lightly the chastening of the Lord, Nor faith when thou art reproved of him; For whom the Lord loveth he chasteneth, And scourgeth every son whom he receiveth" (12:5-6, Phillips). He continues, "Bear what you have to bear as 'chastening'—as God's dealing with you as sons. No true son ever grows up uncorrected by his father. For if you had no experience of the correction which all sons have to bear, you might well doubt the legitimacy of your sonship. After all, when we were children we had fathers who corrected us, and we respected them for it. Can we not much more readily submit to the discipline of the Father of men's souls and learn how to live?" (Heb. 12:5-9, Phillips)

There is another light in the darkness. *We learn great lessons from the reverses of life.* Often, the benefits that accrue to us when we make mistakes more than offset the inconvenience because of our errors. Have you ever heard how blotters came into existence? Man at one time used fine sand to dry the written page. An employee in a large paper mill carelessly omitted one of the ingredients in the writing paper. Apologetically, he told his employer. When the executive tried to write on the paper, he noticed the way the ink ran. A new use for the paper was suggested. A mistake was used to bring a larger good. The suffering of the righteous can mean greater glory for someone else in some other place. Remember that Jesus suffered— although he was without sin. His redemptive love and suffering still bless the world. An old cliche says: "If you succeed without suffering, it is usually because someone has suffered before you. If you suffer without succeeding, it is probably in order that someone may succeed after you."

A third truth helps us. *The present condition is not the last chapter.* We haven't seen all of this life yet, and none of us has seen the life to come. An overbearing and nonreligious farmer said to his neighbor: "I planted my crops on Sunday and cultivated them on Sunday. You went to church and I didn't. Yet, look at our crops. This fall mine are abundant, and yours are mediocre. How do you explain it?" The Christian replied, "God doesn't settle all his accounts in October." Give God a few years! The fog might soon lift and your best days be just ahead. God can restore even the years that the locusts have eaten.

You may, however, have to wait until adjustments are made in the world to come. There's much about heaven we do not know, but the Bible writers tell us it is a place where God "will wipe away every tear . . . and death shall be no more, neither shall there be mourning nor crying nor pain any more" (Rev. 21:4). Our present distress is temporary and rather trifling when we realize what is in store for us. Paul wrote, "In my opinion whatever we may have to go through now is less than nothing compared with the magnificent future God has in store for us" (Rom. 8:18, Phillips). The poet says:

> I know there are no errors
> In the great eternal plan
> And all things work together
> For the final good of man.
>
> And when my soul speeds onward
> In its grand eternal quest,
> I shall say as I look earthward,
> "Whatever was—is best."
> —ELLA WHEELER WILCOX

Why do the wicked prosper? Why do the righteous suffer? They don't always! But, when they do, have faith. God's "got the whole wide world in his hands."

7. Do You Agree with God?

"Do two men travel together unless they have agreed?" (*Amos 3:3, NEB*).

There is something thrilling about being independent! The free-lancer cares nothing for the opinions of men but has perfect liberty to declare what he believes to be the whole counsel of God. Let us remember, however, that if we want to be a harsh critic, like Amos, we must pay the price he paid—a short ministry and few friends.

One of the greatest "loners" in the Bible is this man Amos. He was from the small town of Tekoa, six miles south of Bethlehem and twelve miles south of Jerusalem. The location was most unpromising—desolate wastes and gullies with little water or vegetation! For miles in every direction not another settlement could be found. Only strong, hardy men dared the hills. This outpost of civilization demanded that men wage constant war with the hardness of the desert.

As Amos tended his flock and harvested the desert sycamore fruit, he pondered much concerning the wealth and luxury of the cities in Israel. He had seen some of it firsthand on trips to market and had heard of more from fellow travelers who had journeyed farther north.

What's in a Call?

God does not speak to any two men the same way. Isaiah's call came amid the flying fiery creatures accentuating the holiness of God. To Hosea, God's voice came amid the crushed and pathetic tragedy of a broken marriage. The Lord spoke to Micah amid the cries of his oppressed countrymen. But to Amos, God's summons was imprinted upon the heart that ached and throbbed as the prophet realized his nation needed a restatement of the nature and character of God. The people had substituted ritual for righteousness and had developed the twisted thinking that God could be "bought off" by performing the externals of religious ceremony.

Amos spoke twice of his call. Once was when he warned the people of the destruction that was imminent because of their sins. At that time, he became carried away with himself and forgot he had no "ecclesiastical immunity." He shouted: "The high places of Isaac shall be made desolate, and the sanctuaries of Israel shall be laid waste, and I will rise against the house of Jeroboam with the sword" (7:9). The old-timers used to speak of "personating" someone. Amos "personated" the king, calling him by name. Amaziah, the priest, ran to the king and reported. Later, he hurled at Amos words as caustic as anyone ever spoke to a prophet of God, "Get out, you silly dreamer! Run away to Judah, Earn your bread and make your prophecies there. You shall no longer prophesy at Bethel—Here is the king's holy place, and here his royal palace!" (Amos 7:12-13, Phillips).

Perhaps the "unkindest cut of all" is to accuse a preacher of preaching for money. Amos defended his call: "I am neither a prophet nor the son of a prophet. I am a shepherd and I tend sycamore trees. But it was the Lord who took me from herding my little sheep, and . . . said to me, Go and prophesy against my people Israel" (7:14-15, Phillips). Amos was no professional; he was a prophet because God called him. Man could not put him out of the ministry, because man had not put him into the ministry!

The other mention Amos made of his call was in a series of illustrations showing cause and effect (3:3-8). Two men walk together because they have made an appointment to walk. A lion roars because he has a prey. The warning trumpet sounds and the people are afraid. Every effect has a cause. Likewise, God does not act without revealing his purpose through his prophets. "You see me speaking," says Amos. "It is because God has spoken to me. If a lion roars, who can refrain from fear? If God speaks who can refrain from answering his call?" Amos was preaching *because God had called him and for no other reason.*

A Privileged People

No nation has ever been more blessed than ancient Israel. Yet, few people in history have been so unaware of their spiritual need! David brought prosperity to the land. Solomon and his successors put the country back into a serious economic recession with reckless spending and costly wars. Jeroboam II restored Israel to affluence through military conquests. Amos preached during the latter part of Jeroboam's reign.

Prosperity is devasting to a nation's spiritual life and growth. Goethe said, "Everything in the world may be endured except only a succession of prosperous days." One is seldom prudent enough to resist the effects of good fortune and luxury. Sophocles said:

Seeing upon how slippery a place

> Fortune for mortals and misfortune stand,
> The man who lives at ease should ever look
> For rocks ahead and when he prospers most
> Watch lest he suffer shipwreck unawares.

Israel had become puffed up with a sense of her own importance. She was quite convinced that her prosperity was due both to her superior godliness and her formal religious observances. Because the nation was prosperous, the people had complete apathy concerning moral and spiritual issues. The situation was one of the "blind leading the blind."

Into this sea of tranquillity and content, Amos waded with both fists flying. In the first two chapters of his book, we hear him bringing serious charges against six of Israel's neighbors. Syria, Philistia, Phoenicia, Edom, Ammon, and Moab are singled out for reproof because of their wickedness. The prophet names the characteristic sins of each—the one that seemed to describe that nation particularly. Israel enjoyed this kind of preaching. She did not even become suspicious when he turned upon Judah. This was even better! But then suddenly, without warning, he pointed his finger at Israel.

> Look, I will make you groan in your tracks beneath my weight,
> As the sheaf-covered earth groans beneath the weight of the loaded cart!
> Swiftness of foot will prove no escape,
> The strong man's strength will avail him nothing,
> And the fighting man will not escape alive.
> The archer will not stand his ground,
> And the fleet of foot will not run clear,
> Nor will the horseman make his escape.

In that day the bravest warrior will take to his heels,
And run away, stripped and unarmed!
This is the order of the Lord
                              (Amos 2:13-16, Phillips).

The Prophet's Defense

Such preaching must have stirred the people. A man of
controversy is always a disturbing influence. Those who love
the things of the world do not enjoy being told that the
love of riches leads to emptiness and self-destruction. Someone must have questioned his call. "What are you doing
here? You're not one of us. We're doing all right. Look
at our wealth! Isn't this proof of God's approval! We don't
believe in prophets here in Israel! They are all right for
Judah, but we have our own priests—this is Amaziah's
parish. Go home, country boy!"

Would Amos go? Never! He reminded them of the special
privileges that had come to Israel and then warned that
high privileges always involve more serious responsibilities.
When Israel sins, her guilt is greater—therefore her punishment also.

Amos began his defense with a question, "Do two men
travel together unless they had agreed?" (3:3, NEB) He
pushed the cause and effect argument further as we saw
a moment ago. The question, however, will not leave us,
but haunts continually. Politics may temporarily make
strange bedfellows, but continuous fellowship is contingent
upon agreement in basic principles. Opposites may temporarily attract. They may even supplement weaknesses, but
long-range companionship requires similar likes and dislikes.
Two can walk together permanently only if they share
common interests and goals.

It is Moffatt who gives one of the best interpretative translations of Amos' question. "Do men travel together unless they plan for it?" (3:3) The background is the uninhabited forests which were dangerous. Animals and robbers could snuff out a man's life quickly if he walked alone. He must have company—not merely for fellowship but for safety. If two men were walking together in the desolate area of Amos' home there was only one reason for it—they agreed to it—made a previous appointment. It was no mere accident. The effect had a cause.

Do You and God Agree?

Have you and God had a meeting of the mind concerning the true meaning of life? This begins with a new birth. Many explanations and illustrations of the salvation experience challenge our minds—and our hearts. One of the most stimulating is that which says we identify ourselves with Christ when we receive him as Savior. We accept his way of life as our own, and we renounce as a guiding principle anything that is inconsistent with the Master's approach to true values. This is indeed a "birth from above." The first appointment is for a changed heart. Have you made this initial commitment of "agreeing with God"?

There is much more! A young college student, a beautiful young lady, and a radiant Christian, was asked by a reporter, "What is the greatest lesson you have learned in your church training?" She replied, "I have learned that conversion is but the first step in a lifelong process of Christian growth." The initial decision is a prerequisite. Until we are born again, we cannot begin to grow. But all the remainder of the Christian life is growth—agreeing with God concerning what is essential and what is merely optional.

One other word needs to be said! We do not grow by a mere imitation of Christ. It is by participation with Christ—by letting him work through us. This means surrender to his will. A great Christian once said, "I learned a great lesson the day I discovered that it is not so much what I do for Christ that counts. It is when I surrender to his will and let him work through me that life takes on meaning."

Washington Gladden wrote these words:

> O Master, let me walk with Thee
> In lowly paths of service free;
> Tell me Thy secret, help me bear
> The strain of toil, the fret of care.
>
> Help me the slow of heart to move
> By some clear, winning word of love;
> Teach me the wayward feet to stay,
> And guide them in a homeward way.
>
> Teach me Thy patience; still with Thee
> In closer, dearer company,
> In work that keeps faith sweet and strong,
> In trust that triumphs over wrong.

Do you agree with God? Have you made an appointment with him and are you keeping each appointment regularly through prayer, Bible study, and personal dedication to his purposes for you?

8. What Is Man?

The Psalms are weather-beaten, but they are also eternal. Like the Corinthian columns and other classic works of art, they embody forms of lasting beauty. This beauty is not artificial—the writers did not use cosmetics to stimulate emotions. The Psalms are enduring because they voice human experience realistically and furnish a language for the soul. Rollin Walker says that the man who has learned the Psalms has built for himself a great cathedral in which to worship.

God's True Glory

Psalm 8 is often misunderstood. Its purpose is not merely to present the glory of God in nature. Neither is its purpose to present the glory of man. Its primary purpose is not even to foreshadow the coming of the Messiah. Rather, this psalm presents the true glory of God as being reflected in his making a creature who, although insignificant and puny, possesses dignity and worth.

The "autographs" of God are everywhere. William

Stidger speaks of God's presence in the lightning stroke of every dawn, in the glacial stars and planets, and in the order and unity of the universe. Most of all, however, we see the greatness of God in the crown of his creation—man. The last stanza of Stidger's poem "God's Autographs" says:

> Then to complete creation's plan
> In His own image God made man,
> And signed His name with stroke most sure,
> Man is God's greatest signature.[1]

Many Definitions

Through the centuries man has had mingled emotions about himself. On the one hand he has considered himself to be lower than nothing—a minus zero. One hymn writer calls himself a "worm" while Bernard of Clairvaux said: "Man is nothing else than . . . a sack of dung, the food of worms." Thomas Carlyle called man "a foolish baby." Wentworth Dillon labeled him a "thoughtless animal"; W. S. Gilbert described him as "nature's sole mistake"; while Edward Young concluded man is "the smallest part of nothing."

All, however, have not been so pessimistic about man. William Gladstone said: "Man himself is the crowning wonder of creation; the study of his nature the noblest study the world affords." Actually, man only *appears* insignificant. His rounded brow speaks more than the arched sky, his eyes shine out deeper things than stars, and in his lips there is music beyond that of wind or wave. Less bright than the sun, less bulky than the planet, less abiding than the stars, he is greater than them all! Perhaps the most classic expression from the literary world of man's worth is found in Shakespeare's *Hamlet:*

> What a piece of work is man!
> How noble in reason!
> How infinite in faculty!
> In form and moving
>   How express and admirable!
> In action how like an angel!
> In apprehension how like a god!

Since man cannot make up his mind what he believes about himself, he remains in Niebuhr's words "his own chief problem." Robert Burns said it well:

> Good Lord, what is man? for as simple as he looks,
> Do but try to develop his hooks and his crooks!
> With his depths and his shallows, his good and his evil;
> All in all he's a problem that must puzzle the devil.

What the Bible Says

Do the Scriptures help us with the problem? Realistically, the Bible presents both sides of the question. Man is a sinner. The imagination of his thoughts are evil. The wicked are estranged from the womb and go forth speaking lies. David said, "Behold, I was brought forth in iniquity, and in sin did my mother conceive me" (Ps. 51:5). Paul paints a terrible picture of man in the Roman letter:

> None is righteous, no not one;
> no one understands, no one seeks for God.
> All have turned aside, together they have gone wrong;
> no one does good, not even one
> Their throat is an open grave,
> they use their tongues to deceive.
> The venom of asps is under their lips.

Their mouth is full of curses and bitterness.
Their feet are swift to shed blood,
and in their paths are ruin and misery,
and the way of peace they do not know.
There is no fear of God before their eyes

(Rom. 3:10-18).

On the other hand, the Bible writers believed also in the great potential of man. He is created in the image of God. Sin has marred the image but has not destroyed it. Man possesses a dignity and status not given to any other of God's creatures. He possesses a moral judgment and a capacity for spiritual fellowship. Knowing the trauma of guilt, he also can know the joy of forgiveness. Man does not merely possess a soul. He *is* a soul and knows the meaning of eternal life. The cynic may speak as did Byron of man as

half dust, half deity,
Alike unfit to sink or soar

but the Christian knows better. We are

Not made that our souls in sin should rust,
And God's purpose forever miss;
Not made to be buried in the dust,
But to rise to heights of bliss.

Made to commune with God himself
And with Him forever be,
Not made for the trifling things of time
But to live for eternity.

—AUTHOR UNKNOWN

God Has Blessed Man

If we were to attempt a list of things God has done for

67

man, we would soon realize the impossibility of the task. The psalmist said: "Bless the Eternal, O my soul, / remember all his benefits; / he pardons all your sins, / and all your sicknesses he heals, / he saves your life from death, / he crowns you with his love and pity, / he gives you all your heart's desire, / renewing your youth like an eagle's" / (Ps. 103:2-5, Moffatt). To compute accurately all God has done for man is simply impossible.

For one thing, he has *made* us. Although God uses the creative system which he has ordained for physical reproduction, it is still true that every birth today is a creative act of God. The psalmist said: "It is he that made us, and we are his; we are his people, and the sheep of his pasture" (Ps. 100:3). The skeptic may say, "Man is a highly-developed vertebrate, a more or less clever and successful ape, who has worsted his competitors in the struggle for existence." But the Christian knows better! Man is a creation of God and, therefore, greatly blessed. The cynic may say: "Man is a vapor, a breath that passes away . . . a bubble upon the wave . . . here today, gone tomorrow, gone forever. Man is but one of nature's many experiments and is to make way by and by for another and perhaps a greater. Man has no destiny beyond that which he pictures to himself in his own fancy." But the Christian knows better! He reads: "God created man in his own image, in the image of God created he him. The Lord God formed man of dust from the ground, and breathed into his nostrils the breath of life; and man became a living being" (Gen. 1:27; 2:7). Man is a creation of God.

God has done something else for man. He has *bought* him. Sin entered into man's life, and God sent his Son to buy man back—to pay the price for his sins. Many attempts have been made to analyze and illustrate the meaning of Christ's death on Calvary. The most effective explanation of the atonement is still that of substitution. Jesus died in our place. Do you remember the story of the little boy who made the boat with his own hands. While he was sailing the boat, it slipped down the stream and was gone—the boy's handiwork was lost. Later in a town nearby he saw his boat in a store window. In order to get it, he had to buy it back—he had to pay a price. After purchasing it, he walked down the street with the boat in his hand, talking to it: "You're mine, little boat, you're mine! You're mine twice! Once because I made you! And second because I bought you! You're mine, little boat, you're mine!"

Not only has God made us and bought us, but God *watches over us with his providential love.* There is a verse in the book of Lamentations which reminds us of his goodness. "It is of the Lord's mercies that we are not consumed, because his compassions fail not. They are new every morning: great is thy faithfulness" (Lam. 3:22-23, KJV). The Bible teaches us that God's angels hover round about us and minister to us. His love and protecting hand is real. John Greenleaf Whittier wrote,

> I know not where his islands lift
> Their fronded palms in air;
> I only know I cannot drift
> Beyond His love and care.
>
> Oh, brothers! if my faith is vain,
> If hopes like these betray,
> Pray for me that my feet may gain
> The sure and safer way.
>
> And Thou, O Lord! by whom are seen,

Thy creatures as they be,
Forgive me, if too close I lean
My human heart on Thee!

Many times we would make a mess of things, but God's
providential care keeps us from "dashing our foot against
a stone." How comforting and reassuring, as James Russell
Lowell wrote, to know that in every hour and moment of
need

Standeth God within the shadow
Keeping watch above his own.

God has indeed done much for man!

What God Expects

Since God has done so much for man, he expects much
from man. We are not saved by works, but when we are
saved the changed life produces good works. The psalmist
asks, "What shall I render to the Lord for all his bounty
to me?" (Ps. 116:12) The answer is that we should first of
all, take the cup of salvation that he offers. In other words,
we need to receive Jesus as our personal Savior and become
a born-again Christian. Having done this, we should seek
to be dedicated Christians in the fullest sense of the word.
This means recognizing Christ as Lord in every area of life
and seeking to serve him faithfully every day of our lives.

Can we do any less than this? When we consider what
he has done for us, surely we must respond with dedicated
lives. Elizabeth Barrett Browning once wrote:

What can I give thee back, O liberal
And princely giver, who hast brought
  the gold
And purple of thine heart, unstained

> untold
> And laid them on the outside of the
>   wall
> For such as I to take or leave withal,
> In unexpected largesse? Am I cold,
> Ungrateful, that for these most manifold
> High gifts, I render nothing back at all?

Since God has done so much for man and expects so much from man, man is of great worth. Perhaps man's greatest worth is found in the fact that God has chosen to reveal himself to the world through a man. When we think of space travel and the possibility of life on other planets, we often speculate if they have received revelations of God. We wonder if they could have received a revelation that might be higher and beyond the revelation that we have received in Jesus Christ. It seems, to us, impossible that God could have revealed himself in any way that is superior to the revelation that he has made when God became man. Alice Neynell insists that we cannot tell what other forms of revelation God might choose for other worlds. We cannot guess his secret dealings with other dwellers in his wide universe. She does, however, suggest

> O, be prepared, my soul!
> To read the inconceivable, to scan
> The myraid forms of God those stars unroll
> When in our turn, we show to them a man.

God believes man is important. He is a sinner. He must be born again. But man has great potential. With God's help, man can attain great heights. God is mindful of him and God has done much for him. He also expects much from him.

9. What Do You Do More Than Others?

"What more are you doing than others?" (Matt. 5:47).

Whatever interpretation one places upon the birth of Jesus, his miracles, or the theology that grew up as a result of his life, death, and resurrection, one thing is certain. He is the greatest teacher who ever lived. The way of life that he advocated has been the inspiration for more books, speeches, and institutions of humanitarianism than any other person who ever lived.

Actually, what did Jesus teach? What did he really think was most important? If he were to come back and visit our churches today, what would he think of our programs and priorities? How closely have we caught his spirit, and how near are we to doing in our churches and personal lives the things he taught were essential?

The Sermon on the Mount

Chapters 5 through 7 of Matthew are called the Sermon on the Mount. Scholars are still debating whether this was one sermon actually delivered in a historical situation or whether Matthew has gathered all the main teachings of

Jesus together and constructed a literary vehicle by which to summarize the basic message of Jesus. Personally, this writer prefers to accept it as a definite sermon in a definite place at a definite time. The fact that fragments of this sermon are repeated elsewhere during the ministry of Jesus does not militate against Matthew 5—7 being a unity. Teachers and preachers often repeat themselves.

This sermon has been designated by various titles. F. B. Meyer calls it the "design for happiness." Hersey Davis says it contains the "characteristics of the kingdom man" while Leo Eddleman speaks of it as a "formula for lifting Christians to higher ground." Eddleman says: "No mere man could or would have formulated such principles. The first time you *read* them you feel sure they will not work; the first time you *try* them you know nothing else will work. They call for perfection in yourself but demand that you make allowance for imperfection in others. To read them creates a holy ambition to walk the upward way." [1]

Superior to the Law

The first main division of this sermon has to do with the happiness of a Christian. Several stages of his experience are mentioned. First, a Christian is conscious of his spiritual poverty. Next, he is sincerely sorrowful. Then, he becomes meek enough to be teachable. He hungers and thirsts for the righteous way and, as a result, becomes merciful because mercy has been shown to him. Becoming pure in heart, he, therefore, has no side aims or ambitions—he is *single* in his dedication. He attempts to introduce others to the peace that he has experienced. In holding firm to the standard of righteousness, however, he is often mistreated but rejoices for he knows that he is in the will of God. Such a man is happy. He is to be congratulated for he has found the true meaning of life. Jesus likens such people to salt which purifies and preserves the world. They are light for the world's darkness, and urged to "shed light among your fellows, so that, when they see the good you do, they may give praise to your Father in heaven" (Matt. 5:16, NEB).

The remainder of Matthew 5 shows the superiority of the Christian way of life to that of the one who merely seeks to fulfill the law. The follower of Jesus is not merely one who does not kill. He does not even hold hatred in the heart. Neither is he one who merely refrains from adultery. He thinks no impure thoughts but lives in such a way that his simple yes or no is accepted at face value without any vocal crutches to support his affirmations or negations. The law says "an eye for an eye," but the Christian will not resist evil or seek revenge. He loves all men, both friends and enemies, and follows the example of God who sends life's necessities indiscriminately upon the good and evil alike.

A prominent sociologist has suggested that there are three attitudes toward civil law. First, there is the one who lives in violation—he is a lawbreaker. Second, there is the one who lives up to the point of the law's demands but no further. He takes advantage of every possible loophole for personal gain but will not do anything that would put him in a position of jeopardy. Third, there is the one whose life is pitched on such a high level that he does not even need a law to regulate his conduct. He literally lives "above the law." These same attitudes apply with reference to one's attitude toward God's laws. The Christian, however, is living under the "law of love." He does not try to find a "minimum morality" but seeks to go the second mile in every relationship of life.

Two Striking Questions

As Jesus concluded the section concerning the law, he asked two striking questions: first, "For if you love only those who love you, what credit is that to you?" (Matt. 5:47, Phillips). Second, "And if you exchange greetings only within your own circle, are you doing anything exceptional?" (Matt. 5:47, Phillips). The second question is followed by the pungent comment, "Even the pagans do that much."

These questions underscore the truth that the Christian's life must be superior to the non-Christian's if he is to reflect the spirit of Jesus. One writer said the early Christians won great numbers of converts because they "out lived, out loved, and out died" the pagan people in their midst. The King James Version phrases the second question significantly. It says, "What do ye more than others?"

A Word of Caution

At this point, we must be careful. The Christian is not in a race to outdo others in religious performance. Jesus made this plain in a number of places in his teachings. For instance, he told a parable aimed at those who prided themselves on their own goodness. Jesus said:

> Two men went up to the temple to pray . . . [one] prayed thus: "I thank thee, O God, that I am not like the rest of men, greedy, dishonest, adulterous. . . . I fast twice a week; I pay tithes on all that I get." But the other kept his distance and would not even raise his eyes to heaven, but beat upon his breast, saying, "O God, have mercy on me, sinner that I am" (Luke 18:10-13, NEB).

75

Do you remember the comment of Jesus? After stating that the second man went home justified, Jesus added, "For everyone who exalts himself will be humbled; and whoever humbles himself will be exalted" (Luke 18:14, NEB).

Zeal for the Lord can become so much self-projection that it is egomania. The difference is the matter of our motive. The popular black philosopher, Hambone, said it well, "The world will be a lot better when people start trying to be good and quit trying to be better than somebody else." A businessman once told the writer that for several years he had a great zeal for soul-winning. He said: "I became overbearing with others in an effort to 'win them to Christ.' One day I took a good look at myself and saw that I was actually seeking to dominate them with my own personality instead of winning them to the Lord. I almost lost my faith until I was able to be completely honest and purify my motives." He continued: "I don't have the loud, verbose, self-centered approach to soul-winning now that I once had, but I believe I am coming nearer to the spirit of Christ in leading others. At least, I've learned a great lesson. I hope I'm a better Christian. I am working with a boy's group in church, and I'm trying to love those kids with an unselfish love rather than trying to use them to solve my own emotional problems."

An Essential Requirement

Christians must be different! The supreme test of one's doctrine is the difference that it makes in his character—his daily life. If we would win people to Jesus, we must convince them by showing a better quality of life. The early Christians did not win great numbers of converts merely by what they said. Rather, it was the superiority of their character—their kindness, unselfishness, integrity of life—that convinced the pagans there was something different in being a Christian. James Hastings says: "It wasn't the . . . assertion of the resurrection that wrought this great wonder of history primarily. No; the thing that impressed the world was the Risen Life shining through." Jesus asked, "What do ye *more* than others?" It is this "more" by which the world judges us. What difference does it make in our daily life that we wear the name *Christian?* Are we bearing the name in vain (that is, without it meaning anything vital in our lives) or has his loving presence changed our attitudes, motivations, and actions?

> There's a sweet old story translated for men,
> But wrote in the long, long ago;
> 'Tis the Gospel according to Mark, Luke and John,
> Of Christ and His mission below.

> Men read and admire the Gospel of Christ,
> With its love so unfailing and true;
> But what do they say and what do they think
> Of the Gospel according to you?

> 'Tis a wonderful story this Gospel of love
> As it shines in the Christ life divine;
> And oh, that its truth might be echoed back
> In the story of your life and mine.

> Unselfishness mirrors in every scene
> Love blossoms in every sod;
> And back from its vision the heart comes to tell
> Of the wonderful goodness of God.

> You're writing each day a letter to men

Take care that the writing is true;
It's the only gospel that some men will read,
It's the gospel according to you.
                    —AUTHOR UNKNOWN

An incident from the life of General Chiang Kai-shek challenges us. The incident occurred during the early years of his life while he was liberating China. In connection with one of his campaigns, a hospital was destroyed. The doctor in charge of the hospital asked for the privilege of going with the general and taking care of the wounded men in his army. The general was amazed. "Why would he want to do this when it is because of my campaign that the hospital, his life's work, has been destroyed?" His aide replied, "It is because he is a Christian." Chiang Kai-shek was impressed. "If being a Christian would cause him to do that, I must give more careful attention to my study of Christianity." Those who knew the general closely say that this was one of several incidents which, on the human side, were responsible for his conversion to the Christian faith.

The dear Lord's best interpreters
Are humble human souls;
The gospel of a life like his
Is more than books or scrolls.

From scheme and creed the light goes out
This saintly fact survives;
The blessed Master none can doubt
Revealed in holy lives.
                    —JOHN GREENLEAF WHITTIER

10. What Are You Looking For?

"Then what did you go out to see?" (Matt. 11:8, NEB).

One of the most colorful characters to walk across the pages of the New Testament was John the Baptist. Few men have had his courage, loyalty to God, and uncompromising devotion to truth. Yet he was one of the humblest men who ever lived. When some tried to arouse a spirit of jealousy in him by pointing out that his disciples were leaving him to follow Jesus, he replied, "He must increase, but I must decrease" (John 3:30).

John's ministry had one great purpose. He was to be the forerunner of Jesus, and his preaching was to prepare the way for the Lamb of God—the One taking away the sin of the world. John was the first prophet after nearly four centuries without prophets. F. B. Meyer speaks of him as the "Morning star, shining amid the brightening glow of dawn . . . answering across the gulf of three hundred years to his brother prophet, Malachi, who had foretold that Sunrise and the healing of His wings." Jesus was emphatic and definite in his praise of John: "I tell you this: never has there appeared on earth a mother's son greater than

John the Baptist" (Matt. 11:11, NEB).

Discouragement Comes to All

All men, however, have their periods of discouragement and depression. How John's soul must have thrilled the day he baptized Jesus, and God's Spirit testified: "Thou art my Son, my Beloved; on thee my favour rests" (Mark 1:11, NEB). This divine approval upon John's ministry should have given him enough inspiration to last a lifetime!

But a few months later John was in prison. In times of inactivity, we often lose assurance. John sent two of his disciples to ask Jesus: "Are you the one who is to come, or are we to expect some other?" (Matt. 11:3, NEB). Jesus did not answer the question directly with yes or no. He merely pointed to the results of his ministry—blind people see, lame walk, lepers are cleansed, the dead are raised to life, even the underprivileged have the highest joy of hearing the gospel preached. He then said for the two disciples to tell John that a man is happy if he is not embarrassed because of his relationship with me. In essence, Jesus was saying, "I am all that you said I was—trust me and find peace for your troubled heart."

What a terrible thing it is to be discouraged! Yet all of us have our periods of disillusionment and frustration. David was victorious as he defeated Goliath, but shortly after that he fled from Saul's army and complained that all men were seeking his life. Elijah, with God's help, single-handedly defeated the prophets of Baal but was soon fleeing from Jezebel. He ended up under the juniper tree insisting that everyone except him had forsaken God. Jeremiah was a popular young preacher during Josiah's reign. When the dark days of persecution under Jehoiakim came, however, he complained that life was not worth living. If you have not had your period of heartbreak, it is coming—perhaps soon. But God will see you through. Longfellow wrote:

Be still sad heart and cease repining
Behind the clouds is the sun still shining.
Thy fate is the common fate of all
Into each life some rain must fall,
Some days must be dark and dreary.

The Comment to the Crowd

After the messengers from John had gone back to report, Jesus turned to the crowds. No doubt, many of them had heard John. Perhaps, some had been devoted to him. He asked: "What did you go out to the desert to see? A reed swayed by the wind . . . a man arrayed in soft raiment . . . a prophet?" (Matt. 11:7-9, Moffatt).

What was Jesus saying? Was he not asking, "What was it about John that attracted you to him?" How closely our worship of God is bound up with the one who leads us in the worship! Why is this true? Is it not because he interprets God to us and brings us face to face with the essential elements of divine truth?

And from your eye He beckons me
And from your heart His love is shed
Till I lost sight of you and see
The Christ instead.

This question of Jesus is for all of us. Why do you go to church? What do you expect to get out of the worship service? What, in your opinion, are the essential elements in a person that make him a spiritual leader? What elements are important to you in character building? What basic

81

philosophy of life is yours in spiritual ideas and ideals?

A Shaken Reed

There are two possible meanings for the phrase "a shaken reed." First, it was a kind of proverb. It meant "the commonest of sights" and referred to the long cane grass which grew down by the banks of the Jordan River. By this, we would interpret Jesus to mean: "When you went to see John were you merely going to see something as ordinary and mediocre as reeds swaying in the wind? Is this all your religious life means to you?"

More likely, however, Jesus was using the "shaken reed" illustration to indicate a weak vacillator. William Barclay describes the picture as "one who could no more stand foursquare to the winds of peril than a reed by the river's bank could stand straight when the wind blew." Too many people are like this—weak, inconstant, easily swayed by the wind of popular favor and applause. Such people are always siding with the party in power. Never found in the ranks of a small minority, they are never thermostats—only thermometers. They serve as weather vanes and reflect the temperature but never help determine it. Such people have no principles. They merely have opinions and can change them to please anyone with whom they find themselves associated at a given moment.

The "shaken reed" life is an aimless one. Having no real purpose, it shifts from one goal to another. R. C. Campbell once described such a life in his story of the dog who started to run a deer. Soon, he left it to chase a fox. Next, he decided to trail a squirrel. Then, he began to run a rabbit. Finally, he was pursuing a field rat. All around him was a forest with an abundance of game, but he ended up barking into a rat hole. Campbell says, "Many lives are like that—no aim, no direction, no perseverance." The important question is not where you are now but rather where you are going.

Clothed in Soft Raiment

The pioneer spirit so easily gives way to love of luxury and sophistication. Too often in life this happens! We work hard in our youth for security. We, however, misunderstand its meaning. To the average man, security means a time when he can relax with the assurance that he shall have no economic problems or worries. He can have material advantages, even a plush way of life.

This view of life overflows into one's religious philosophy. In the early years of a church's life, the people struggle to provide a place of worship and facilities for the educational and recreational program. The church is interested in people. No sacrifice is too great to make in order to reach families with the gospel of Christ. But, somewhere along the way, the people change their sense of values. They become more concerned with ease and comfort than with the sacrifice that is necessary for disciplined living. Churches, in many cases, find themselves wanting to resemble "country clubs" rather than Bible teaching institutions and places for spiritual worship.

Love of ease will prove fatal to an institution or an individual. This is our problem as a nation, and it is spilling over into our church life. One present-day minister says: "Too many of our people are ease loving, pleasure loving, money loving. They are being lured by the voice of pleasure and the greed for gold. Nations that feed on pleasure and gold are destined for desolation." The same is true of churches and individuals. Do you remember the experience of the great general, Hannibal? He spent one winter with his army engaging in luxurious living. They turned themselves loose to all the inclinations of the flesh. What all the snows of the Alps and the hot suns of Italy could not do to Hannibal's army, one winter's ease and indulgence did. It was stripped of discipline, lost its power, and was plunged into ruinous defeat. Those who love ease and luxury, at the price of dedication, compassion, and concern, are doomed for destruction.

A Prophet

What did the people see in John? They saw a man of God—a prophet. In popular usage today, we have come to designate a prophet as one who can foretell the future. Actually, this was only one part of his work in biblical days. A prophet was one who spoke to the people of their spiritual need. His message was relevant to the actual conditions under which the people were living at that time.

Prophetic preaching is the kind which is conscious of the activity of God in every situation. The prophet believes God has a word for the present generation. He is the living God and is at work in the lives of people. The truth the prophet declares is timeless—valid for every generation because it is the unchanging word of God. The principles of life which the Old Testament prophet declared were relevant for his day, but they are also relevant for our day because they reflect the character and moral demands of an eternally holy God.

Today's world has many needs. The greatest, perhaps, is for our churches to get off the defensive and launch a great spiritual offense for Christ. We have become content to eke out a bare existence on spiritual pabulum. Too long the church has listened to the world. We need to realize we have a message for the world, and it is the world who needs to be listening to us, not us to them! A recent magazine article had accompanying it a picture of the Colosseum in Rome. The article spoke of it as a place "where early Christians died for a faith the world now takes for granted." God has not called for us in our generation to *die* for the faith, but he is calling for us to be *living* witnesses.

> So he died for his faith. That is fine
> More than the most of us do.
> But stay. Can you add to that line
> That he *lived* for it, too?
>
> It is easy to die. Men have died
> For a wish or a whim—
> From bravado or passion or pride.
> Was it hard for him?
>
> But to live: every day to live out
> All the truth that he dreamt,
> While his friends met his conduct with doubt,
> And the world with contempt.
>
> Was it thus that he plodded ahead,
> Never turning aside
> Then we'll talk of the life that he led,
> Never mind how he died.

What do you look for in a church? Let the church be the church. We are still in business for one reason—to introduce people to Jesus. This was John's mission. It is ours, also.

11. What Is Life Worth?

"For what will it profit a man, if he gains the whole world and forfeits his life? . . . What shall a man give in return for his life?" (Matt. 16:26).

Several years ago a number of newspapers printed a note of a young girl who committed suicide. It said: "I am twenty-one. I have seen everything worth seeing. I know everything worth knowing. I don't like life—it's cheap, dirty, disappointing. I've had all I want."

About this same time, the papers also told of a banquet held in Ontario, Canada, in honor of Sir William Mullock who was ninety-five years of age. He had served in Parliament, had been chief justice of the supreme court and vice-chancellor of the University of Toronto. A number of speeches were made honoring him. As he arose to acknowledge the stirring applause, he spoke with a firm and clear voice. A man who loved life, cared for people, and enjoyed work, he said: "I am still at work with my hand to the plow, and my face to the future. The shadows of evening lengthen about me, but morning is in my heart. The testimony I bear is that the Castle of Enchantment is not yet behind me. It is before me still, and daily I catch a glimpse of its battlements and towers. The best of life is always further on. Its real lure is hidden from our eyes, somewhere behind the hills of time."

What was the difference between these two people? Was it not the difference in understanding the true purpose and meaning of life's worth?

Finding Life's Meaning

Who is the happiest person in the world? Not the one who has the most material possessions or the highest position of prestige but rather the one who has found purpose in life. Ralph Waldo Emerson said: "Life is hardly respectable if it has no generous task, no duties or affections that constitute a necessity of existence. Every man's task is his life-preserver."

Of course, this task must be a worthy one, challenging the highest and best within the person. Often our aims are too easily obtainable. They are not worthy goals. A pastor was once boasting that his church pledged the entire budget the first Sunday of the stewardship campaign. A good layman replied, "Did you ever think that perhaps your goal was not high enough if you did it that easily?"

What is the true meaning of life? What kind of goals should we have? Too many of our hurried and busy activities have too little to do with the real issues. We are rather similar in our modern living to Artemus Ward's description of his lectures. He said, "You know one of the chief characteristics of my lectures is that they contain so many things that have nothing whatever to do with the subject." Is this not a commentary on most of our busy lives? True meaning is found in depth, and depth is found in caring for the needs of others. John Ruskin wrote: "He only is advancing in life whose heart is getting softer, whose blood is warmer, whose brain quicker, and whose spirit is entering into living peace. And the men who have this life in them are the true lords and kings of the earth—they, and only they."

The Master's Challenge

Jesus was never guilty of giving a cheap and easy invitation. He believed service was the supreme purpose in life. To him, true greatness came through giving of oneself to worthy causes. He explained to his disciples that he must go to Jerusalem and suffer death. Peter rebuked him and insisted this should not happen to him. Jesus said to Peter: "Away with you, Satan; you are a stumblingblock to me. You think as men think, not as God thinks" (Matt. 16:23, NEB).

Yet today we still think too often, as Peter thought. We picture the Christian life as a joyride, not as a disciplined journey. We love prestige and status. Jesus tells us, "If anyone wants to follow in my footsteps he must give up all rights to himself, take up his cross and follow me" (Matt. 16:24, Phillips). Three simple thoughts are in these words of the Master. First, put self on the cross. Second, put the cross on self. Third, put the cross in action. Let us, however, remember the true meaning of the cross. It is not that which we are called on to suffer against our wills nor the painful thing we wish we could escape. Our cross is that task we have voluntarily accepted in life as our service to mankind's need because we love Jesus and want to continue his work on earth through our life. This may—and probably will—involve difficulty and even suffering, but it is done willingly for the sake of our Savior and his kingdom. This is true living. The poet Francis Quarles wrote:

> The way to bliss lies not on beds of down,

And he that has no cross deserves no crown.

Each of us must face the matter of what he shall decide in life are the true values. If we place self first, we shall never discover our true self. We find fulfillment in life only as we live completely for the cause of Christ—which is a life of service for others. Jesus said: "Whoever cares for his own safety is lost; but if a man will let himself be lost for my sake, he will find his true self" (Matt. 16:25, NEB).

> I want in this short life of mine
> As much as can be pressed
> Of service true to God and man
> God helps me do my best.

Profit and Loss

No businessman wants to operate in the red. In fact, he cannot afford to do so very long. Neither should we want our lives to be wasted—a total loss. Yet, often we stay right on the borderline. It seems as though we try to operate on a "minimum morality" basis—just close enough to be nominally Christian, but not enough to be truly committed. We are much like the man whose bookkeeper came to him and said: "Boss, I've got good news! We're out of the red. It's close, but we showed a small profit last month. But there's one problem. We've operated in the red so long we don't have any black ink. What shall I do?" The boss replied, "That's easy. Take some money out of petty cash and buy some black ink." The bookkeeper said, "There's another problem. If I do, we'll be back in the red."

When is life wasted? Jesus tells us that it is when a person seeks to gain security for self and ignores spiritual values. He says: "For what good is it for a man to gain the whole world at the price of his real life? What could a man offer

89

to buy back that life once he has lost it?" (Matt. 16:26, Phillips).

Shortly after World War II, Billy Rose wrote a provocative article in the *New York Times*. He told of nine of the wealthiest men in the world who were present twenty-five years before at a meeting at the Edgewater Beach Hotel in Chicago. Among them were the presidents of the world's largest steel company, the world's largest utility company, and the world's largest gas company. Also present were the greatest wheat speculator in the world, the greatest "bear" on Wall Street, and the head of the world's greatest monopoly. A member of the President's cabinet, the president of the Bank of International Settlement, and the president of the New York Stock Exchange completed this list of nine men.

Most of these men had been described as "success stories," and young people had been urged to follow their examples in planning their lives and careers. Collectively, these men owned or controlled more money than there was in the United States Treasury. Yet twenty-five years later, what had happened to them? Two had become bankrupt. One had died abroad, penniless and a fugitive from justice. One had gone insane. Two had been recently released from prison and three had committed suicide. John A. Mackay, Presbyterian missionary pioneer, said, "Life does not begin at twenty-one or at forty or seventy. It begins when one is captured by something bigger than a selfish self-interest—an idea, a person, a cause, to live for and die for."

> We all are blind until we see
> Within the human plan
> That nothing is worth the building,
> If it does not build the man.

And why build we cities glorious
If man unbuilded goes?
In vain we build our buildings,
Unless the builder also grows.
—EDWIN MARKHAM [1]

Are You Winning or Losing?

You may be saying: "I agree we should not sell out ourselves to the riches of the world. Those who pile up wealth
at the sacrifice of principles are foolish. I'll never be guilty."
But what about the ideals and ambitions of your life? The
poet said:

It's not what you'd do with a million,
If riches should e're be your lot;
But what are you doing at present
With the dollar and quarter you've got?

If you are not concerned with the needs of others now,
it is very doubtful that you would be if you had ten times
as much. Those who remain unconcerned, it is true, seem
to save themselves considerable expense—both in time and
money. At the end, however, they slip out of life similar
to the man of whom Charles Lamb wrote, "He passed away,
dying as he lived, without much trouble." Let no one,
however, fool himself. This kind of life is not a victorious
life. It is a defeated one. Thomas Gibbons wrote:

That man may last, but never lives,
Whom much receives, but nothing gives;
Whom none can love, whom none can thank—
Creation's blot, creation's blank.

Have you heard of how Charlemagne, the mighty warrior
and emperor, was buried? His body was placed in a vault.

A sword was placed in his hand, and an open Bible was at the base of the statue. The point of the sword was stretched down and touched the Bible. Some time later it was noticed that the point of the sword was lying on the verse which said: "For what shall it profit a man, if he shall gain the whole world, and lose his own soul?" (Mark 8:36, KJV)

What will it profit, when life here is o'er
    Though great worldly wisdom I gain,
If seeking knowledge—I utterly fail
    The wisdom of God to obtain?

What will it profit, when life here is o'er
    Though gathering riches and fame,
If, gaining the world—I lose my own soul
    And in Heav'n unknown is my name?

What will it profit, when life here is o'er
    Though earth's farthest corners I see,
If, going my way, and doing my will
    I miss what His love planned for me?

What will it profit, when life here is o'er
    Though earth's fleeting love has been mine
If, seeking its gifts—I fail to secure
    The riches of God's love divine?

What will it profit? My soul, stop and think
    What balance that day will declare!
Life's record laid bare—will gain turn to loss,
    And leave me at last to despair?
                                        —GRACE E. TROY

12. What Is a Saved Man's First Prayer?

"And he trembling and astonished said, Lord, what wilt thou have me to do?" (Acts 9:6, KJV).

In his novel, *Mr. Britling Sees It Through*, H. G. Wells says: "Until a man has found God and been found by God, he begins at no beginning, he works to no end. He may have his friendships, his partial loyalties, his scraps of honour. But all these things fall into place and life falls into place only with God." The Bible uses a number of metaphors and other illustrations to describe what happens in this experience. It is spoken of as a "new birth," a "passing from death to life," "becoming a child of God," and being "redeemed through his blood." One of the most meaningful of all, however, is that a person is "saved."

According to the New Testament, the word *salvation* has a threefold sense. We are *saved* when we become a child of God. We are *being saved* as we grow in grace and knowledge of our Lord. We *shall be saved* in the glorious consummation of his coming again. In the first experience, we are saved from the *penalty* of sin. In the second, we are saved from the *power* of sin. In the third, we are saved from the *presence* of sin. To be realistic, however, we usually use the word *saved* and *salvation* in religious conversation to refer to the first of the three experiences—that of becoming a Christian. Perhaps it is because, subconsciously, we feel there is more urgency in one's becoming a Christian than in growing in the Christian graces.

Saul and Stephen

Let no one think that it all happened to Paul in an instant on the Damascus road! It had begun much earlier! Saul was present when Stephen was stoned. He never forgot the experience of seeing Stephen dying. But there was something else! The unanswerable sermon of Stephen haunted his theological mind. Saul of Tarsus was a scholar. He knew that the arguments and logic of Stephen made sense.

It was no accident that immediately after the stoning of Stephen the persecution became more violent. Nothing drives an aggressive bigot to greater zeal for a cause than for him to have a gnawing at his conscience that his opposition is right and he is wrong. Much of our loud vocalizing is trying to convince, not others, but ourselves. Notice such expressions as: "Saul harassed the Church bitterly. He would go from house to house, drag out both men and women and have them committed to prison" (Acts 8:3, Phillips), and, "Meanwhile Saul, still drawing his breath hard from threatening and murderous desire against the disciples of the Lord, went to the high priest" (Acts 9:1, Amplified Bible). Saul was restless. He was kicking "against the pricks."

Many scholars think Saul and Stephen engaged in a number of debates in the synagogue at Cilicia. They believe Stephen confounded Paul in logical arguments and so infuriated him that he plotted to kill Stephen. One poet has put words into the mouth of Saul in his debate with Stephen as he gave his concept of the Messiah,

> Be sure that when he comes
> His high degree will shine
> Illustrious like the sun in him;
> Not feebly flicker for your fishermen
> From Galilee to point it out to you.

But Stephen held no such interpretation of Old Testament Scriptures. He saw the spiritual implications of the Old Testament messianic passages. He answered with "love all aflame" in such a way that his words were

> A vivid weapon edged with flame
> And in those hands so wielded,
> That its stroke no mortal might abide.
> —AUTHOR UNKNOWN

This may be mere creative imagination of the poet, but one thing is certain. Saul saw Stephen die. He never forgot it. Stephen's prayer had much to do with the conversion of Saul.

Saul's Conversion

An old truism says, "Its always darkest just before the dawn." The period of persecution, led by Saul, was a dark hour for Christianity. He dominated the scene. No one was his equal in ability, training, or experience. Someone has suggested that Christianity might have been stamped out if it had not been for the conversion of Saul of Tarsus. Of course, this is an overstatement. These "ifs" of history can never be known for certain, but Saul was unquestionably a serious threat to the existence of this young movement. God, however, was in the shadows keeping watch above his own. When the wolf went forth against the sheep, the Good Shepherd touched the wolf and made him a meek little lamb.

When did the actual conversion take place? Before we answer this question we might consider Barclay's striking words: "This is not a sudden conversion; but it is a sudden surrender . . . in the moment the long battle was over and Paul surrendered to Christ. So into Damascus he went a changed man." A. T. Robertson raises the question as to whether Saul was converted on the Damascus Road or after his eyes were opened in Damascus. He then says: "The matter is not very material but one is led to conclude that the surrender took place during the interview with Jesus. . . . He surrenders on the spot. . . . There is no reserve. He is the slave of Jesus from this time forth. . . . He had seen the face of Jesus before he fell to the earth and darkness came over him."

Regardless of when the moment of change came, it did come, and Saul was never the same. He was like that later Christian who spoke of his experience, "I took one look at him, and he took one look at me, and behold we were one forever." Stephen had left his mark on Saul. Now Saul was ready to take up his unfinished work of preaching spiritual religion to a group who were enmeshed with the shackles of legalistic approach to righteousness and morals. Moreover, his experience has become one of the greatest and most unexplainable miracles of the Christian faith—second only to the resurrection of Christ.

A number of years ago two outstanding agnostics ventured forth to disprove the validity of Christianity. One was to explain away the resurrection of Christ—the other the conversion of Saul. They considered these to be the two bulwarks of the Christian faith. After a long period of research, each became convinced of the integrity of the biblical accounts and became Christians. So will everyone who is genuinely objective in attitude and completely thorough in study.

What does this story teach us? Paul used it as an object lesson—a test case—of the power of Jesus to transform the most hardened of sinners. Alexander Maclaren says: "The conversion of Saul shows that there are no helpless cases, and bids us to be sure that no heart is so hard but that the love of Christ can soften it."

Proof of Conversion

What is the test of whether or not a man has been saved? It is not mere intellectual assent to the fact of God. James wrote: "You have faith enough to believe that there is one God. Excellent! The devils have faith like that, and it makes them tremble" (Jas. 2:19, NEB). Neither is it the fact that one has had an emotional experience concerning his shortcomings. This is not to deny the importance of sorrow for sin nor to imply that emotion in conversion necessarily means instability. Neither is the criterion of conversion one's willingness to identify himself with an institution—the local church. This is a good decision—essential for the most meaningful and effective service—but church membership of itself is not a proof of conversion.

What is the proof? Is it not when one is willing to ask, as Paul, "Lord, what wilt thou have me to do?" Of course, merely to ask the question is not enough. One must be willing to do that which God reveals to be his will. The saved man is the one who is completely subservient to the will of Christ—the complete lordship of Jesus—in every

97

area of life and practice. James Moffatt points out that when Saul called Jesus of Nazareth "Lord" he was using the Greek word which translated the awe-inspiring, unpronounceable "Yahweh" (Yhwh) of the Old Testament. In other words, in that moment Saul had accepted Jesus as the risen Christ, King of kings and Lord of lords. He had placed Jesus of Nazareth on the throne of his heart and accepted him as the full and complete revelation of Yahweh—the Creator and Sustainer of the universe.

> Because his hand set planets in their courses,
> And scooped the bed where rolls the restless sea,
> Because he leashed the winds and stacked the hills,
> Because his presence makes the darkness flee;
>
> Because he bade the lame to rise and walk,
> Because he heard a desperate beggar's call,
> Because he clothes the lilies of the field,
> And stoops to mark the smallest sparrow's fall;
>
> Because he broke death's chains and banished fear,
> Because his love has filled my soul with peace,
> He is my glorious Saviour, Lord and Friend,
> He is my King whose reign shall never cease.

Have You Asked?

Now, let us consider a personal matter. Have you asked the Lord the question Paul asked? Up until the moment of his conversion, Paul had been doing the things he thought best—*that which he wanted to do.* His own will had dictated his way of life. Now it would be different! He would make every choice in the light of God's will for him. Is this not the true meaning of being saved? William Barclay puts it very simply yet strongly, "The Christian is a man who has

98

WHAT IS A SAVED MAN'S FIRST PRAYER?

ceased to do what he wants to do and who has begun to do what Jesus Christ wants him to do."

Have you begun this way of life? Is your real purpose in living for Jesus to live all over again in your life? Paul expressed his great desire, "I passionately hope . . . the greatness of Christ will shine out clearly in my person, whether through my life or through my death" (Phil. 1:20, NEB). Many definitions have been given of Christian consecration but here is one of the best: "Consecration is signing your name at the bottom of a blank sheet of paper and letting God fill in the rest."

An editor gives us a great lesson concerning the use of our ability. He noticed that an outboard motor was doing nothing most of the year, and it disturbed him. Think of all that horsepower going to waste! He set his imagination to work! He designed a three-wheeled scooter with handlebars and a seat. He also designed a tank containing antifreeze to serve as a cooling agent. He commented that experience shows us that people, as well as machines, function best when they are employed close to full potential.

It is mind-staggering to contemplate what would happen if more persons would use their creativity to put their God-given abilities to capacity use instead of letting them lie idle on the shelf. If we would do so, we could eliminate from our lives the spiritual rust that accumulates when we work lazily or not at all. Have you asked, "Lord, what wilt thou have me to do?" This should be a saved man's first prayer. The hymn writer Mary Brown expressed it thus:

> There's surely somewhere a lowly place
> In earth's harvest fields so wide,
> Where I may labor thro' life's short day
> For Jesus the Crucified;

So, trusting my all unto Thy care,
I know Thou lovest me,
I'll do Thy will with a heart sincere,
I'll be what You want me to be.

13. What Do You Think of Your Church?

"Or do you despise the church of God?" (1 Cor. 11:22).

One of our modern ministers tells of a small church close to the English coast that was destroyed in a hurricane. The congregation delayed rebuilding because of financial inability. One day a representative of the British Navy asked the minister their plans. The pastor explained their problem. The officer replied: "If you do not rebuild the church, we will. That spire is on all our charts and maps. It is the landmark by which the ships of the seven seas steer their course." What a parable for us in our day! In a time when people are falling apart, the message and guidance of our churches are needed as never before if we would find security, strength, and stability.

The Church at Corinth

No other church gave such a variety of problems to Paul as the one at Corinth. For this reason, his first letter to the people deals with a variety of subjects—divisions concerning spiritual leaders, sexual immorality, legal disputes between church members, problems concerning marriage and divorce. He included the matter of proper types of food to be eaten, hair styles for worshipers, women speaking in church, exercising of spiritual gifts, observance of the Lord's Supper, speaking in unknown tongues, death, and resurrection.

Do you remember the founding of the church? Paul had just left Athens where he was laughed out of the city by the intellectuals. It seems that he had tried a new approach—one different from the straight exposition of Old Testament Scriptures as at the other cities. The new approach was sophisticated but it had one drawback. It was sterile. James Stewart says, "Moonlight preaching ripens no harvest." A few seemed impressed by Paul's message but not enough to start a church. Whether we like to admit it or not, Paul was far from a success at Athens!

When he came to Corinth, he made a new resolve. He would return to the old gospel. As he wrote back to the church later he said: "As for me, brothers, when I came to you, I declared the attested truth of God without display of fine words or wisdom. I resolved that while I was with you I would think of nothing but Jesus Christ—Christ nailed to the cross" (1 Cor. 2:1-2, NEB). Paul's meaning seems clear. He did not try to attract the Corinthians with the cleverness of his mind or the brilliance of his intellect as he seemingly sought to do at Athens. He had learned what Longfellow later expressed:

> It is the heart and not the brain,
> That to the highest doth attain.

This kind of preaching brought results! It always will! A church was established at Corinth with vitality and aggressiveness. The church was, however, as cosmopolitan as

102

the city. Two ethnic groups comprised the congregation. There were Jews who were thoroughly saturated with Old Testament law. They were, however, the minority group. Gentiles, converted to Christianity directly from paganism, made up the larger section. They were unfamiliar with the disciplines of Old Testament morality—in fact sexual activity was a familiar feature of the pagan worship rites. The Temple prostitutes were not only uncondemned, but they were considered as dedicated individuals! No wonder Paul had problems with this young church!

Fellowship in Worship

One by one he suggested solutions for the problems. Let the people grow up and quit worshiping leaders instead of God! Let them realize their body is a temple for the indwelling of God's spirit! Let them realize liberty in Christian living should not be perverted until it becomes a license for the gratification of every personal whim or every desire of the lower nature! Let them realize that a Christian must forego some harmless indulgences for the sake of the kingdom of God! Then Paul came to the matter of fellowship in the body as pertaining to worship and also as related to social life among the members.

The Corinthians had originated a beautiful service called the "love feast." It was a fellowship meal in which each brought food as he could afford. They then sat down and ate together. For some of the poor people, including the slaves, it was a particularly delightful occasion. It was for many of them the only decent meal during the entire week. Gradually, however, the sharing was lost. The socially privileged ate their food in little exclusive groups ignoring the underprivileged. Barclay says that the thing that should have

103

been a beautiful fellowship had "degenerated into a series of class-conscious cliques."

This perversion of the love feast disturbed Paul greatly. He rebuked them severely for both their actions and attitudes and criticized them sharply for their factions and favoritisms. These selfish cliques were a hindrance to the gospel. He described their activity: "When you meet together . . . in eating, each one goes ahead with his own meal, and one is hungry and another is drunk. What! Do you not have houses to eat and drink in? Or do you despise the church of God and humiliate those who have nothing? What shall I say to you? Shall I commend you in this? No, I will not" (1 Cor. 11:20-22).

The Place and Importance of Churches

Paul is asking the Christians at Corinth what they think about the importance of their church. Is it a place where they come for worship and Christian fellowship? This is what it should be! Is it a place where the spirit of Christ dwells? If our worship today degenerates into empty and meaningless activity, the world will become contemptuous of our churches and their programs.

There is much prejudice today against what is called the "institutional church." Many people are saying the churches have failed and other organizations and groups will arise and take the place of the churches. This claim is not new. People have said this in every generation. Of course, the churches have their shortcomings. So do people! But the churches are all we have. Let one try to imagine the kingdom of God functioning on earth without the churches. To conceive of such a possibility is actually ludicrous. An old truism says, "I'm not much, but I'm all I've got." We may be disappointed with people, but who would suggest depopulating our planet because of the imperfections of human beings? A cynic may describe our churches today as the lines William Watson said:

Outwardly splendid as of old
Inwardly sparkless, void, and cold
Her force and fire all spent and gone—
Like the dead moon, she still shines on.

But many of us know better. We know the churches may have seen their duty imperfectly since they are made up of fallible people. After all has been said, however, it is the churches that have preached the gospel of Christ and have stood for moral standards, unselfish service, and spiritual religion for twenty centuries. We still can sing, even in a confused and bewildered world:

I love thy Church, O God!
Her walls before Thee stand,
Dear as the apple of Thine eye
And graven on Thy hand.

For her my tears shall fall;
For her my prayers ascend;
To her my cares and toils be giv'n,
Till toils and cares shall end.
—TIMOTHY DWIGHT

Whether the hymn writer was speaking of the universal body of Christians or the local churches, the truth applies to every Bible-believing congregation in a meaningful way.

Do You Love or Despise Your Church?

Of course, the church *belongs to Jesus.* He established

it and said to Peter, "On this rock I will build my church, and the powers of death shall never conquer it" (Matt. 16:18, NEB). We sing the words written by Samuel J. Stone:

The church's one foundation
Is Jesus Christ her Lord;
She is His new creation,
By Spirit and the Word

But is there not another sense in which each of us calls the church to which he belongs "my church"? We are committed to it and have invested ourselves in it. There is no real inconsistency in calling it Christ's church and in the same moment calling it "my church." Existentially, it is both!

Is it correct to say there are many people who despise the church today? Let us look closely at what Paul meant. The word he used when he asked, "Despise ye the church of God?" is the Greek word *kataphroneo* which means literally "to think down." This word has the suggestion of "condemn," "scorn," "think in disparagement of." This is exactly the attitude which many people in the world today are taking toward the churches. Let us be realistic about it! Some adopt this attitude as a camouflage for the real problem—they have rejected the life and character for which the churches stand. Some, however, are sincere in feeling that the churches are failing in their ministry. They, too, might be spoken of as "despising the church" in that they fail to appreciate the full significance and importance of her mission in the world.

This modern attitude, however, is nothing new. In every generation, redemptive and social ministry groups spring up, and people predict these will replace the ministry of the local institutional churches. There was a time when some people proclaimed loudly that the YMCA would replace the churches and their programs. Others felt this way about the Salvation Army and the Red Cross. In our generation we have seen many independent, nonchurch-related youth movements arise and make meaningful contributions. But none of these good organizations will replace the churches.

Do you love your church—the one to which you belong? There are many good causes which we may support with our influence, our energy, and our money. Some things are good but other things are better. When one invests himself in the work of the Lord through his church he is choosing the best channel—the one which will do the most constructive and effective work in the community and the world. If one would profess to believe in justice but not courts, to believe in healing but not hospitals, to believe in education but not schools, we would regard him foolish. To organize ideals into working institutions is difficult, but it is ridiculous to pretend we believe in these ideals and run away from the attempt to make them work in a concrete and realistic situation.

Do you love your church? After all of the nonchurch-related causes have been analyzed and evaluated, the work of the churches still stands as the most effective and enduring. Are you giving your best in support of your church? A minister once made a terrible mistake at a funeral. As the remains of the departed lay in the casket before the pulpit, he said, "This corpse has been a member of my church for ten years." Many people mean just about as much to a church as a dead corpse. One man became convicted about this truth and said:

I've been a dead weight for many years,
Around the church's neck
I've let the others carry me,
And always pay the check.
I've had my name upon the rolls,
For years and years gone by;
I've criticised and grumbled too;
Nothing could satisfy.
I've been a dead weight long enough,
Upon the church's back
Beginning now, I'm going to take
A wholly different track.
I'm going to pray and pay and work,
And carry loads instead;
And not have others carry me
Like people do the dead.

—AUTHOR UNKNOWN

Of course, there are no perfect churches. Who has ever claimed that there are any? Neither are there any perfect people or perfect homes or perfect schools. But we can strive to make our church—the one to which we belong—better in fellowship, in service, and in doing the work of Christ upon earth. One person wrote:

I think that I shall never see
A church that's all it ought to be;
A church whose members never stray
Beyond the straight and narrow way;
A church that has no empty pews;
Whose pastor never has the blues,
A church whose deacons always "deak"
And none are proud, and all are meek:
Where gossips never peddle lies,
Or make complaints or criticise,

Where all are always sweet and kind,
And all to others' faults are blind,
Such perfect churches there may be,
But none of them are known to me.
But still I'll work and pray and plan
To make our own the best we can.
                    —AUTHOR UNKNOWN

Do you love or despise ("think down on") your church?

14. Four Questions with the Same Answer

"If God is for us, who is against us? . . . Who shall bring any charge against God's elect? . . . It is God who justifies; who is to condemn? . . . Who shall separate us from the love of Christ? (Rom. 8:31,33-35).

One of the favorite poems of many people from childhood is by an unknown author entitled "Mr. Nobody." Do you remember how it goes?

I know a funny little man
As quiet as a mouse
Who does the mischief that is done
At everybody's house
There's no one ever sees his face
And yet we all agree
That every plate we break was cracked
By Mr. Nobody.

'Tis he who always tears our books
And leaves the doors ajar
He pulls the buttons from our shirts
And scatters pins afar
That squeaking door will always squeak
For naturally, you see
We leave the oiling to be done
By Mr. Nobody.

The finger marks upon the door
By none of us are made
We never leave the blinds rolled up
To let the curtains fade,
The ink we never spill
The boots that lie around you see
Are not our boots, they all belong
To Mr. Nobody.

Did you know there is a section in the Bible containing four questions that can all be answered with the same word—nobody. The questions are found in Romans 8:31, 33-35. Each of these questions is important for victorious and happy living.

A Marvelous Chapter

Romans 8 should be read and studied not only with great gladness but also with profound reverence. Few chapters contain such rich material concerning the relationship of the Christian to his Lord. One expositor speaks of this chapter as beginning with "no condemnation" and ending with "no separation." The work of God's Holy Spirit is emphasized in this chapter as much or more than any section of the New Testament.

Paul spoke of the "law of the Spirit of life in Christ Jesus" and contrasted this with the "law of sin and death." "Walking after the Spirit" was contrasted with "walking after the flesh." Those who are led by the Spirit of God are the sons of God and his Spirit bears witness with our spirit that we are God's children. Paul wrote of the Spirit helping us with our weaknesses and making intercession for us in our time of need. It is no wonder this chapter is called "that great chapter which sets forth that part in our salvation

111

which is exercised by the third Person of the Godhead."

God and Our Good

It is in this chapter that we find the glorious verse concerning how God works seemingly adverse circumstances for our ultimate gain. Most of us remember this verse and can quote it from the King James Version which says, "And we know that all things work together for good to them that love God" (Rom. 8:28, KJV). The RSV, however, gives a fresh and much needed insight, "We know that in everything God works for good with those who love him." Do you see the difference? It is not "things" that work—it is God who works things.

One of man's greatest needs is to remember constantly that God is still "working things." He has not abdicated his sovereignty nor forfeited his leadership. It is still God who "has made us" and we are still "sheep of his pasture." The metaphors of other centuries may not be stimulating to some modern minds. Some people may seek for more creative expressions to define our relationship to the divine. The further honest scholarship goes in serious study, however, the more scholars find their way back to the great "I am." One outstanding scientist, after years of study, confessed, "I'd rather believe all the follies and fables of fairyland than to believe for one moment that this world is without a Universal Mind." Most of us see no intellectual contradiction in calling this "universal mind" God and accepting Jesus Christ as his highest revelation. We believe he is a God of love who is working for our good.

Who Can Oppose Us?

Paul's first question is, "If God be for us who is against

112

us?" This is a question that faces us every day. Do we really believe God is on our side—that he has our best interest at heart? There are certain laws that are written into the very constitution of the universe. They are for our good. The real difference between people is not circumstances but their response to and attitude toward circumstances. Put one man in prison, and he grows bitter—feeling he is mistreated. Put another in prison, and he sings praises at midnight or writes *The Pilgrim's Progress*.

Eve's problem in the Garden of Eden is so often our problem. When Satan said: "Did God say," and, "God knows that when you eat . . . your eyes will be opened, and you will be like God, knowing good and evil" (Gen. 3:5), Eve began to doubt God's love for her. This is the same attitude of the spoiled child with a snarling attitude who says "my parents—in fact, all adults, are against me." One of the surest marks of maturity is when we come to recognize that others, including God, are not plotting against us.

What about the question and its answer? No one can be against us if God is for us. That is, no one who matters. Any opposition which might arise, because we have taken a stand for God, is insignificant when compared to the assurance that we have his approval. If God loved us enough that he did not hesitate to give his Son for us, can we not trust him to supply every need when problems arise?

Who Can Accuse Us?

The matter of our sin and guilt is always present with us. The second and third questions deal with this matter. The fundamental teaching of the New Testament is that God has dealt with the guilt of our sin when Christ died on the cross. The matter of whether we die and go to hell

113

is settled when we accept Christ as personal Savior. This is not the only benefit accruing from Christ's sacrifice, but it is the first and most important. Remove this truth from our theology and we have only an anemic gospel—a mere humanism with no vitality or dynamic.

Paul asks, "Who shall bring anything against God's elect?" The answer is nobody. Paul reminds us that it is God who justifies the ungodly. Paul is using a figure of speech from the courtroom. Lawyers have an expression "once in jeopardy." This means if a person has once stood trial for a crime and been declared "not guilty," he can never be tried for that crime again. This is the premise upon which the gospel message is built. Paul says: "Therefore, since we are justified by faith, we have peace with God through our Lord Jesus Christ" (Rom. 5:1). William R. Newell says: " 'Peace' means that the war is done. 'Peace with God' means that God has nothing against us . . . God has fully judged sin, upon Christ, our Substitute . . . God was so wholly satisfied with Christ's sacrifice, that He will eternally remain so: never taking up the judgment of our sin again . . . God is therefore at rest about us forever . . . God is looking at the blood of Christ, and not our sins . . . All claims against us were met when Christ made peace by the blood of His cross."

Who Can Condemn Us?

The third question is similar to the second. Paul asks, "Who is to condemn?" The answer is nobody. Why? Because Christ is at the right hand of God pleading our case. Our sin has been dealt with "once for all," and we are free from its penalty. A minister once had a dream concerning death. Satan stood before him in judgment with a list of sins. He said, "Are these all my sins?" Satan replied, "Oh no, there are many more." "Bring them to me," he insisted. Satan departed and came back with a number of books, "These are all your sins," he declared. The man said, "Stack them all in a pile and write above them, 'The blood of Jesus Christ cleanses us from all sin!'" Jesus said: "I give them eternal life, and they shall never perish, and no one shall snatch them out of my hand" (John 10:28). The hymn writer wrote:

> The soul that on Jesus hath leaned for repose
> I will not, I will not desert to his foes;
> That soul, though all hell should endeavor to shake,
> I'll never, no, never, no, never forsake!

No one can lay anything to the charge of God's child nor can anyone condemn him. *He has been adopted into the family of God.*

Who Can Separate Us?

The greatest truth about the Christian life is that it is fellowship with God—through Jesus Christ. Beyond a doubt, to know that God loves us is the most meaningful part of a Christian's experience. Take away our certainty of his concern for us and all life crumbles. Paul, therefore, closes this great chapter with a comforting reassurance of God's loving presence.

Who shall separate us from the love of Christ? Paul could have said simply nobody, but he chose to say it in a far more striking manner. He asked, "Shall physical adversity—affliction, hardship, persecution, hunger, nakedness, peril or sword—do it?" The answer to this is that we die daily for his sake, and yet we become conquerors through his love. Paul then lists several categories of occurrences that cannot break the relationship nor mar the fellowship of a child of God with his heavenly Father.

The extremest changes of our condition—life and death—do not affect God's love. Elsewhere, Paul said, "Whether we live . . . and whether we die . . . we are the Lord's" (Rom. 14:8). Again, *no order of beings beyond ourselves*—angels, principalities—can draw him away from us or us from him. Alexander Maclaren reminds us they "may stand beholding with sympathetic joy; they may minister blessing and guardianship in many ways; but the decisive act of union between God and the soul they can neither effect nor prevent." The *power of time*—things present, things to come—are impotent to sever us from his loving care. This is particularly significant when we remember that it is time and space which work so fatally on human love. They, however, have no effect on God's love.

This leads us to the last category. If time cannot affect adversely his love, *neither can space*—height and depth. In fact, it seems Paul had become weary and impatient of enumerating the impotencies. When he named the outside boundaries of the universe—time and space—he flung with rapid toss one final word—any other creature. Notice the artistic arrangement of these phrases. There are a pair of opposites followed by triplets then another pair of opposites followed by triplets. The cumulative effect is to reenforce the greatest truth of the Christian faith—God's ever present love for his own.

These words from the song "Love of God" express this idea.

> Could we with ink the ocean fill,
> And were the skies of parchment made;

Were ev'ry stalk on earth a quill,
And ev'ry man a scribe by trade;
To write the love of God above
Would drain the ocean dry;
Nor could the scroll contain the whole,
Tho' stretched from sky to sky.[1]

One of John Wesley's helpers was once thrown in a dungeon beneath a slaughter house. He said that the scent was worse than a pigsty because of the blood and filth that came into it from above. He added, however, "My soul was so filled with the love of God that it was a paradise to me." God can make us superior to our circumstances. If we "practice his presence" with love, we can be victorious in any situation.

15. What Do You Think of Jesus?

"What do you think of the Christ? Whose son is he?" (*Matt. 22:42*).

Politicians make strange bedfellows! Likewise, two enemies of a good man often find they have temporary agreements! How true it was in the life of Jesus. There was no reason for the groups in Matthew 22 to be aligned with each other except their common hatred for our Savior.

Look at the Pharisees

Does virtue ever become a fault? Can a person be so good that he's good for nothing? Before we seek to criticize the Pharisees, however, we should seek to understand them. Then we should honor them for their major contentions. When we review their background and the principles for which they stood, we can see many fine points about them.

No people of antiquity have been so misunderstood as the Pharisees. They have been considered as monstrosities of evil, and most of us remember little, if anything, about them except that Jesus heaped condemnation upon them. In our ordinary, everyday speech, the word *pharisee* is synonymous with *hypocrite*. People have confessed many

118

kinds of sins, but have you ever known one to confess to being a pharisee?

Look at the beginning of the Pharisees. In the second century before Christ, the Greeks attempted to destroy the Jewish religion. In order to do this effectively, the Old Testament had to be destroyed. According to the apocryphal book of First Maccabees, the Greeks tore in pieces the books of the Law and burnt them with fire. People who were found possessing any part of the Hebrew Scriptures were put to death. The Jews, however, could not tolerate this blasphemy from the Greeks! Judas Maccabaeus led his fellow countrymen in revolt. Out of this background the Pharisees arose. They were determined to preserve Judaism. The Pharisees were the "defenders of the old time religion and faith." Even if their concepts were narrow, we must praise them for their firm and unshakable loyalty to their concept of religion and the revelation of God which they possessed. Perhaps the greatest Pharisee of all was Saul of Tarsus. Until the end of his life, he held tenaciously to some of the good traits of his Pharisaism.

But the fault of the Pharisees was at the very point of their virtue. Their goodness had become hard and mechanical. They lacked a warm heart and tender spirit. Their virtue had crystallized, and they were entirely blind to the fact that in order to remain good we must be continually on the road to spiritual growth. The Pharisee did not need to grow—he already had his religion in a capsule. He was lacking, however, in enthusiasm for helping heal humanity's hurt. The Pharisees were the hard-shelled conservatives of their day. When this happens, righteousness loses its loveliness, obedience becomes legalism, and virtue degenerates to hypocrisy. How good and yet how bad were the Pharisees!

Now, Look at the Sadducees

Most of us have a vague and shadowy idea of the Sadducees. We know that they were the rivals of the Pharisees, but what did they stand for in the first-century controversies?

Although the origin of the Sadducees is not known, we are certain they began shortly before the Christian era as a reaction against the narrow attitudes of the Pharisees. For one thing, they protested against some of the rules and restrictions that had been placed upon life. These rules would have been amusing if they had not been so foolish and dangerous for spiritual religion. For instance, the Pharisees would not allow a woman to look in her mirror on the sabbath day. Why? She might find a gray hair on her head, and what woman could refuse the impulse to pull it out. That would be laboring on the sabbath! Sadduceeism said what old Uncle Remus said years ago, "Don't git me himmed up . . . I wants elbow room."

The Sadducees protested against the national prejudices of the Pharisees. Because one served Moses, did this forbid his reading and even appreciating the Greek philosophers? The Sadducees said no.

Theologically, the Sadducees were liberals. Possessing a nebulous creed, they had no sure word concerning anything. They had thrown off Judaism's orthodoxy as useless luggage that impeded the progress of one's spirit. The tragedy was, however, that they had loosed themselves from the moorings and were adrift on the sea of nothingness. Like the crew in the fable who lightened the ship by throwing away everything including the compass, Sadduceeism made the same mistake that much liberalism makes today. By discarding the great doctrines of the faith, they had run up a blind alley. As Peter Marshall once said, "Unless we stand for something, we will fall for anything."

Who Were the Herodians?

Not a religious sect as such. We can almost see their belief by their name! This group supported the dynasty of Herod, but nothing is known of them for certain beyond what the Gospels tell us. Three times (Matt. 22:16; Mark 12:13; 3:6) they come on the scene. Two of these three occasions are parallel passages in the ministry of our Savior.

Although we cannot state with certainty their political aims, they understood enough about Jesus to know that his pure and spiritual teachings of God's kingdom could not be reconciled with their view of a literal kingdom on earth with Herod's family as the rulers. They were, therefore, the logical ones to ask the question concerning the tribute money.

Wise Replies to Foolish Questions

Jesus would not be trapped in the word game! He refused to join the "either or" crowd but rather identified himself with the "both this and that" group. Give to the state that which belongs to the state, but do not let it under any circumstances interfere with loyalty to God. Twenty centuries have not brought any finer statement concerning the relationship of church and state.

The question concerning the resurrection was equally foolish. Naturally, the Sadducees would ask it since they, along with denying any supernaturalness in religion, scoffed at any kind of resurrection. The illustration was too much! Seven straight brothers die after being married to the same

121

woman! What kind of "Bluebeard in reverse" was she? Jesus ignored, however, the ridiculous illustration and pointed out the scriptural teaching. Relationships in heaven are different!

The third question was not all that foolish. It also came from the crowd most likely to ask it. Which law is the greatest? Of course, the Pharisees would ask that one! The reply of Jesus summarized the minutia of the legal requirements in two striking sentences. Love God supremely! Love your neighbor as much and in the same way that you love yourself! Who could improve on that?

The Master's Turn Comes Next

Turnabout is fair play! The enemies have had their day. Now Jesus demands to be heard. The question is simple, but succinct. What do you think of me!

Actually, our Savior did not use his name but his title. Was he inquiring as to their concept of the Anointed One or was he asking what they thought of him as a man? Probably the former. At least, they understood him that way. They replied that the Christ was the Son of David.

Of course, that was true in a genealogical and biological sense. Jesus came from the house of David. Both Joseph's and Mary's genealogies go back to Jesse's son. More, however, is involved! David spoke of the coming Messiah as "Lord" which implies or rather affirms that the king of national Israel is subservient to the king of spiritual Israel. After that, no one was able to compete with his wisdom.

A Question for Us

The words of Jesus are more than an academic interrogation from long ago. They come echoing down the corridors of the centuries. This question, and its corollary, asked by Pilate (Matt. 27:22) constitute the two supreme confrontations that deity has with humanity. What do you think of Christ? What will you do with Jesus? Upon the answer that we give to these questions hang for us the most momentous issues of life. If Jesus is God and we receive him as Savior, we can, with him, face the darkest hours of life victoriously. If, however, he is only a man—even the best man who ever lived—there are no true answers to the questions of life, the grave, and the world to come.

Who is Jesus? Mahatma Gandhi is reported to have once said that even if Jesus is not the Son of God that the Sermon on the Mount is still true for him. Unfortunately, however, Jesus does not give us such an alternative. He deliberately placed himself at the center of his message. He did not say, "Receive my teachings." But he said, "Receive me!" He did not say, "My message is the light of the world." He said, "I am the light of the world." All other religious teachers have inverted the priorities. They have said, "I am nothing, but my message is everything." Jesus says, "Receive me as a person. When you do this, life falls into proper perspective."

What can I do with Jesus? Not three alternatives but two are before us! We can receive him as Savior and Lord. Whatever the sin or shortcoming, Christ has atoned for it. Whatever the weakness, we can be strong in him. Whatever the failure, victory may be ours through the Lamb. A young lady, conscious of her sin, heard the preacher hold high the standard of righteousness in his sermon. As he pleaded for the people to live up to the requirements set down by the Sermon on the Mount and other teachings of Jesus, the lady forgot herself for a moment and cried out aloud in the service: "But what if we can't do those things? What if we're weak, what if we fall short? Is there any hope?" The answer is a resounding yes to everyone who has sinned and come short. The same Jesus who is our High Priest in glory and exalted above all the created angels was once a human being upon earth and entered into all of the things that tempt us. He, therefore, knows and understands our shortcomings. In the first chapter of Revelation, the face that shines above the brightness of the sun is the same face that on earth drew sinners to his feet. The hand that holds the seven stars is the same hand that while upon earth in the days of his flesh was placed upon the little children to bless them. We can receive this Savior and live for him. But we can do the other also! Mortal man can turn down the sovereign God in Christ. Puny, insignificant man can say no to the Lord of creation.

Does it matter what I do with Jesus? A million times over it matters! In life, in death, in eternity! The best people on earth today are those who are motivated properly by the living Christ. Those who die with ease and assurance are those who have placed their hands in the nail-scarred hand. Those who live throughout eternity with him are those who begin their eternal life with a decision for him while tabernacling upon this earth.

Who will decide the question? You will decide it for yourself, and I will decide it for myself. There are no proxy votes in the matter of our soul's salvation.

> Once to every man and nation
> Comes the moment to decide.

When shall I decide the question? Do it now! Why now? There are at least two good reasons. First, you may die tonight. This is not the highest motive for receiving Jesus, but it is a wise one and a safe one. Again, choose Jesus today because the sooner you become a Christian the sooner you begin to know the joy of walking with him in faith and love.

Can You Prove It?

Faith and reason are not at odds. They supplement each other, but faith is superior. In fact, faith is necessary because, in the final analysis, the best things in life cannot be proved except by participation in them. Jesus was not afraid of the scientific test. He said: "If any of you really determines to do God's will, then you will certainly know whether my teaching is from God or is merely my own" (John 7:17, TLB). This is what faith is all about! Not trying to believe in spite of the evidence, but daring to do in spite of the consequence! Faith is linking one's self with the eternal in a commitment that defies all possible compromise or indifference.

Notes

Chapter 2

1. G. A. Studdert-Kennedy, "Indifference," *Christ in Poetry* (New York: Association Press, 1952), p. 168. Compiled and edited by Thomas Curtis Clark and Hazel Davis Clark.

Chapter 5

1. Henry Van Dyke, "Four Things," *A Treasury of the Familiar* (Chicago: People's Book Club, 1945), p. 654. Edited by Ralph L. Woods.

Chapter 8

1. William L. Stidger, "God's Autographs," *Christ and the Fine Arts* (New York: Harper and Bros., 1938), p. 545. Compiled by Cynthia Pearl Maus.

Chapter 9

1. H. Leo Eddleman, *Teachings of Jesus in Matthew 5-7* (Nashville; Convention Press, 1955), pp. 1-2.

Chapter 11

1. Edwin Markham, "Man-making," *Masterpieces of Religious Verse* (New York: Harper and Bros., 1948, p. 419. Edited by James Dalton Morrison.

Chapter 14

1. F. M. Lehman, "The Love of God," (Nazarene Publishing House, 1917).